Stop Quitting on Yourself

The 5 Rs to Living Your Dreams

Amber Howard

Stop Quitting on Yourself: The 5 Rs to Living Your Dreams
Amber Howard

The author designed the information to represent her opinions about the subjects disclosed. The author obtained the information contained through personal experience and the experiences of her clients and as such does not assume any responsibility for the actions or the results of the actions of the reader.

The author disclaims any liability, loss, or risk incurred by individuals who act on the information contained herein. Personal transformational work can produce strong emotions, if you get stuck or have a sudden negative change in thinking or behaviour that you are unable to resolve for yourself, please seek out a trained professional who can assist you.

Please check with a medical professional before starting any exercise program. The information in this book is not meant to take the place of professional advice.

Contents

Dedication

I dedicate this book to my #1 bestest mom,
your angel wings continue to illuminate my life in
ways I will never fully understand.
You are forever loved and deeply missed.

Love,
Your #1 Bestest Daughter

And to
My dad for instilling in me a work ethic only a farm kid has
and for the support that is never taken for granted.

And to
My children Jada and Edwin, you are the fuel for my soul.

Foreword

The question is not 'if' your life will change after you experience this book; it is WHEN and by how much it will change. I never knew how simple change could be until I read Amber Howard's book, *Stop Quitting On Yourself.* Applying the 5 Rs, as Amber explains in this book, will take you beyond what you thought possible.

Often you set limits on your goals based on the beliefs you currently have, but as you change those unsupportive beliefs, the metaphorical ceiling of your goals naturally rises. Your expectations and results rise because your self-esteem, self-confidence, and self-worth have also risen. Instead of seeing this as a challenge or defeat, the new mindset created after reading this book will have you prepared and ready to meet any opportunity.

The 5 key components Amber outlines in her book make achieving what you want feel not only possible, but also easy. The practical, clear and experiential exercises in this book will guide you to transform your struggles into successful endeavours. You will no longer feel the guilt, shame, and frustration of not reaching your goals.

Amber tells her experiences exactly how you need to hear them, so that your growth and development will be very specific to what you need. Authenticity shines through her words, and you can feel her compassion, understanding and empathy. Her passion and drive to help you surpass your potential is evident in the value and caliber of her work.

Powerful examples and testimonials bring this book to life, to provide inspiration and empowerment. It will feel like you are not left alone to figure it out, as Amber is right there, mentoring you each step of the way. You will discover things about yourself that you were unaware of, and you will be able to use this knowledge to exponentially expand and grow, both personally and professionally.

With the extraordinary amount of advertising you are influenced with every day, this book could not have come at a better time. Stop Quitting on Yourself forces you to look within yourself to reignite your power and potential. Internal motivation creates more results and success than external motivation does, which is a contributing factor to why you feel like you can reach your goals.

Amber guides you on an exploration inside yourself to uncover what it is you truly want before taking one step forward on your path. You could save years of future struggle, heartbreak, and tears by reading this book right now! It is the blueprint for creating a fulfilling life, free from sabotage, triggers, regret and excuses. I recommend this book if you are struggling to make changes in your life.

When I first met Amber, it was overwhelmingly evident that she is passionate about helping you create the life you truly deserve. She is a living example of the teachings applied within these pages. She has personally experienced the feelings of frustration and failure as a result of trying to change without getting results. Amber teaches from her heart, and from years of researching human habits and behaviours. Her book, coaching, and courses provide the opportunity for you to discover who it is you want to be, and bring forth the confidence and resources to achieve your goals. Change doesn't have to be hard, especially when you have this book as a navigational map guiding you on your journey. Follow the 5 Rs to change your life and make your dreams a reality!

Raymond Aaron
New York Times Bestselling Author

Chapter 1

Behind the Struggle

Why People Struggle to Change

Have you ever struggled to quit this, start that, slim down, fix this or solve that? If you are human, chances are there is some habit or behaviour in your life that you are trying to change. It is in our DNA to be driven to evolve and advance. Science has proven that humans are happier and healthier when they are learning and growing. If this is true, why do we find ourselves staying stuck, struggling, sabotaging, and ultimately stopping, on our way to what we say we want?

Unfortunately, we are not taught how to make changes. Schools do not have *Change 101* classes. Our parents struggled with change themselves, so they were not much help in this department. There have been no instruction manuals, Holy grails, or stepping stones to teach us how to change.

Why do we say we want change, only to, more often than not, be right back where we began? Hours, days, months, and in some cases, years of our lives dwindle away as we chase the ever- elusive, disappearing rainbow and its pot of gold. All the sacrifice, blood, sweat and tears seems futile as we find ourselves, once again, back at the starting gate. What is worse than starting over is that self-esteem, self-confidence, and self-worth gets hit hard during the process. So not only are you back doing the same old habits and behaviours, it is easy to start buying into the belief that you don't have the ability to change. Riding the merry go round of motivation and defeat reaffirms the belief that change is hard.

If you judge a fish by its ability to climb a tree, it will spend its whole life believing it is stupid.
– Albert Einstein

But, what if change wasn't really all that difficult? What if it was only a belief that we have been taught so that companies could profit from individuals *stuck* on the merry go round? What if, with the right tools and education, change could be simple and easy?

Weight loss and stopping smoking are two of the biggest markets in demand in North America. Billions of dollars are spent annually on products, services, marketing, and advertising, convincing society that they can't make changes on their own. Industries have created an epidemic with these messages telling us that change is difficult and cannot be done without this or that product. This is further reaffirmed by people *trying* to change without the proper information. Many products advertised are nothing more than a placebo, or simply flat out don't get results. It is no wonder so many people give up and quit on their dreams and goals.

Behind the Struggle

Would you like to know the secret that those billion dollar companies don't want you to know? You hold the power to change, INSIDE of you. The key to your success is INSIDE of you. It is not out there in some pill or gimmick. When you stop looking outside of yourself for an answer, empowerment prevails. This book will assist you in discovering how to tap into your inner power, to create change from the inside out.

When you change the way you look at things,
the things you look at change.
– Wayne Dyer

How many times have you declared that come Monday, you will *no longer this or no longer that?* Next year, I will... When summer comes, it will be easier to... I just need to do this or that first... When this happens, or that happens, then I can make the change I need to... When things slow down, I will have more time to... Sound familiar?

Some will say that we are just creatures of habit, which, as I will explain later, is in fact true. How can being a creature of habit assist you instead of work against you? Wouldn't it be nice to have supportive habits occur automatically without you having to think about doing them—to be able to wake up and be on the treadmill before realizing you are not negotiating with yourself about how many more times you can hit the snooze button before you are late; to happily grab for the veggies in the tray instead of the cookies sitting right there; to walk right past the sale of the year for something you do not really need with a feeling of abundance inside; or to automatically feel calm and serene when your mother in law comes for a visit? This is not a trick, or over-exaggerated marketing; it is absolutely a reality for you, if you choose it. In fact, I am certain you will be giving a lot of one-handed high fives to yourself as you progress through the book. (For those of you unfamiliar with this concept, it is where you slap the palm of your hand on your forehead in an "ah-ha!" moment.)

This book was created to support people who are frustrated, depressed, have lost hope, or have no idea where to start in creating the life they dream of, desire and, most importantly, deserve! Yes – deserve. One of the most common obstacles of someone not achieving their dreams is that they believe they are not deserving of success. Let's get something out of the way right now: YOU ARE WORTHY AND DESERVING! Do you know how I know this? Go ahead and place your fingers on the inside of your wrist. Do you feel that? Thump, thump thump. If you have a pulse, you are worthy and deserving of your dreams. Case closed. Moving on.

If you are ever feeling like a failure,
just remember that YOU were the fastest sperm.
– Unknown

Making the changes required to get the health, wealth, and happiness does not have to be challenging. If you choose to use this book to its fullest potential, you can make your dreams a reality, and maybe even quicker than you thought possible.

Warning! Possible side effects of reading this book AND doing the exercises: You may learn that you dream too small and end up climbing higher. It is possible that negative habits or behaviours that you were not even aware of, or focused on, disappear. You become happier, healthier, and wealthier, even

4

if those were not your original intentions for reading the book. It is also common that people who commit to doing the exercises find that what they thought they wanted is no longer true for them. They uncover a new purpose and vision for their life. After reading this book, you may feel as though you drank a metaphorical kool-aid, and crave more personal awareness and development. Your friends and family may notice that you are more focused and happier. People will find you more attractive and are magnetized to your new vibrant energy. It is likely you will have more energy and accomplish more in a day, as well.

Pretty good side effects, eh? (Oh, yes, I am Canadian, if you didn't know already, or couldn't tell by the 'eh' remark). If these are the side effects, you may be asking yourself, "What is the big takeaway I receive from reading this book?" That is a good question. The answer lies in you. Each person who reads this book will get a different experience. They will get a different experience because the book is not packed full of facts and information for you to memorize or interpret. Reliving high school English classes of analyzing and deciphering what the author did or did not mean, and how it could apply to your life, is not our aim here. Let's face it, we have all listened to speakers, or read enough metaphorical books that are inspiring at the moment but do not really support in creating the change or shift we were after.

This is what you WILL get in this book: You will have the opportunity to engage in life-altering, hands-on activities and exercises. These exercises are designed to light up your core being, get you connected with what you really want, and provide specific tools to get you what you most desire and deserve. The outcome of each activity will vary depending on your openness, your willingness to participate full on, as well as your level of commitment and where you are in relation to where you want to be right now. You will be introduced to practical techniques that support in modifying the way you think, making desired results easy peasy lemon squeezy. Change is largely about changing our inner game to see the results in our outer world. Our body does what the mind tells it to do; therefore, many of the exercises involve creating new ways of thinking.

We are what we think.
– Buddha

First things first: Before we push our sleeves up and get into the juicy stuff, let's make sure you are prepared for the amazing transformation that will occur.

Shocking information ahead!!! In order for change to actually happen, you need to stop at each exercise, and... wait for it.... actually do the activity. I know, I know, it sounds ludicrous. You can print out the activity sheets at www.stopquittingonyourself.com, or use loose leaf to create your own version. If you decide to print out the activity sheets, print them all out at once and keep them in a duo-tang or binder. That way you will have them all in one spot and be able to refer back to certain exercises.

That means, I know, getting up right now and going to print out the activities or get a notebook. I get it. Sometimes it is easier to just keep reading than taking action right now. But, ask yourself, "Where else does this play out in my life?" Is it easier to hit the snooze button than getting up to go to the gym? Is it easier to have the rich dark chocolate brownie than to say no thank you? Is it easier to say I will do it later? Of course!

However, I invite you to consider this statement: How you do one thing is how you do everything.

If you are unwilling to get some paper and a pen right now, you might as well close the book and gift it to someone who is ready and willing to take the necessary steps to success. This may sound a little harsh to you, or it might be the wake-up call you need to become aware of how you keep yourself, your dreams, and your reality, small. Dreams do not generally fall into your lap while you are snuggled up in bed or on the couch. "But I just got tucked into my warm cozy bed." "The computer is all the way downstairs." "If I turn my computer on, I know I will lose at least an hour of my life on Facebook." "I will just keep reading and print out the pages tomorrow." Believe me, if you are thinking of an excuse not to go get the paper right now, I have already used that one. I once even convinced myself that I would just think about my answers instead of writing them down, so as to reduce my environmental impact and save a tree— seriously!

Breezing through the book and briefly thinking about the activity for 10 seconds before you turn the page will not get you the results you are looking for. The reason I know this is because this is what I used to do when I read books with activities in them. I never wrote my thoughts down. I just figured sitting and thinking about the questions for a minute or two would do the trick. I did not need to journal my thoughts as I had them all organized upstairs. Interestingly enough, when I did go back and reread some of the books and do the activities, they were very influential books for me, even if I did sacrifice a tree to do it. Set yourself up for success right now, and get the necessary supplies to support you. Don't worry; the book will be here when you get back.

Waiting...

Did you stop reading to get the necessary supplies? Good for you, if you made that choice. Life is all about making decisions and being the creators of how we want our lives to look. Taking action is a declaration to the universe and yourself that you are committed to your success.

If you are planning on reading ahead without supplies, ask yourself: "Where else does this play out in my life?" Are you a procrastinator? Do you wait until the last minute to get something done or need the pressure of a deadline to get motivated? Do you not really want to change? Are you afraid to be successful? Are you saying you want change, but are not willing to put the effort out to receive results? If you answered yes—perfect! This is the book for you!

> *"I don't have time" is the grown-up version of*
> *"the dog ate my homework."*
> – Unknown

Homeplay: Committed to My Success

This is your first Homeplay exercise. You may be wondering why it is called Homeplay rather than homework. Let me ask you this: What sounds more fun and exciting to do? Homeplay or homework? That's what I thought too!

Each Homeplay exercise throughout this book will outline the approximate amount of time it will take to complete, the purpose of the exercise, materials required, how to complete the exercise, and suggestions of what to do with the awareness and information afterwards.

Time: 5-15+ minutes

Purpose: The purpose of this exercise is to become aware of how confident you think you will be about your commitment to success. Notice it did not say how successful you WILL be, only how confident you THINK you will be. This is an important distinction to note. Remember, the body does what the mind tells it to. If you start out thinking you will not achieve your goals, chances are you will not do the actions required. Awareness is the first step to change!

Materials Required: Paper, Pen, Mirror

Exercise:

Have a pen and paper ready to write down all the thoughts and feelings that come up after you do the exercise. They may be very slight or very intense, and may last for a few minutes or go away as quickly as they flash through your mind. It is essential for you to write the thoughts and feelings down and not just try to remember them. Don't judge or spend time analyzing your thoughts; just write down what comes up for you in the moment. Feel free to write jot notes and short form. There are no extra points for perfectly structured sentences; in fact, I encourage you not to write sentences.

Spend a few moments thinking about what it is that you want in your life and what it will take to realize your goal. Next, stand in front of a mirror. Look yourself in the eyes and pay attention to the feelings and thoughts that show up right after you say the following words *out loud,*

"I am committed to my success."

What feeling do you get in your body? What thoughts automatically come up for you? The feelings or thoughts may be very quick, or may not go away for a few seconds, or even minutes. Repeat the line several times.

Take a few minutes now to organize what you wrote down. You can journal about your experience of the exercise, how you feel afterwards, and what you believe is your take away, lesson, or gift. How are you going to apply what you just learned in your life? What are you going to do with this new awareness?

Takeaway:

Here are some possible reactions to the Homeplay exercise. If you have a little nausea, a sinking feeling in your stomach, and clenching in your chest, or if negative thoughts pop up, you most likely have some fear, or experience some resistance in your efforts to achieve your goals. This resistance can show up as self-sabotage in a variety of forms such as: getting sick or hurt; life getting busy all of a sudden, leaving 'no time' for you to work on your goals; extra, unexpected expenses come up; special occasions throwing you off routine; starting fights or drama in relationships; etc. Basically, any time you make an excuse, procrastinate, overbook yourself, or overthink things, you are self-sabotaging. You often sabotage yourself without even knowing it or recognizing it as that! Don't worry! In this book, you will discover how to become aware of, and recognize, these patterns, as well as what to do to shift out of them, and how to ensure they do not throw you off course.

Some of you may have felt expansiveness, and felt lighter as you spoke those words. This most likely suggests you have positive beliefs that will support you. You have confidence in your abilities and think or feel like you will be committed to your success. It is likely that you will find it easier to take the necessary actions to achieve your goals.

If, for some reason, you think you didn't feel or experience anything, I invite you to redo the exercise. See if doing it with your eyes closed to block out any distractions allows the feelings to be more noticeable. Some people are not used to listening to their bodies, making this observation less intense. This used to be my experience, but with the techniques I will be sharing in the upcoming chapters, you will no longer have this disconnect. Continue to keep practicing, saying this to yourself in the mirror over the next few days, and be open to receiving insights.

The experience you had in this exercise, and all the exercises in this book, was, and will be, perfect for you. The feedback of negative thoughts or feelings only means that you have some underlying beliefs that are working against what you are stating. You will be learning how to rewrite these unsupportive beliefs into positive empowering ones, throughout this book. Receiving feedback is fantastic! Feedback gives you awareness, and that is the first step to change!

Our greatest fear should not be of failure...but of succeeding at things in life that don't really matter.
– Francis Chan

Who is She?

Before I reveal to you the five requirements needed for change to happen easily, automatically, and joyously, there are some things you should know about me. This author is a straightforward, shoot from the hip, call it as it is kinda gal, if you haven't picked up on that yet. I live an amazing life! I am a single mother of two *drive me crazy, love them to bits, wouldn't change a thing about them* children. I spend my days doing what I want. I have travelled all over the world, and I have never been happier. But, it wasn't always this way.

At 29, my dreams of the perfect life were shattered. I was in the throes of a divorce and found myself moving to a new community that was more affordable. The downside was, I knew no one. I thought, "This is it!" I had hit the cold, hard, rock bottom everyone talks about. I remember being told that the good news about hitting rock bottom was that there was nowhere to go but up. What a crock that turned out to be!

As if being a single mother with a two year old and being eight months pregnant with no support network in a new community wasn't enough stress, my mother, who was my best friend, babysitter, and whole support system, was diagnosed with terminal cancer. My stress was off the charts. Trying to control a busy two year old while breastfeeding with mastitis at heated lawyer meetings sounds comical looking back, but it was my reality. I was constantly being torn between learning to be a single parent, tending to my children, working full time teaching high behaviour needs teenagers, and driving the two hours home to spend time with my dying mother. Those drives were some of the hardest moments in my life, not knowing whether

I would ever see or talk with my mom again and making every attempt possible to hide my sadness and depression from my children. Every trip home was a stressful balancing act— keeping an infant and toddler quiet so my mother could rest, trying to find the right words to talk to my mom, and the strength to reassure her that everything would be fine—while, all along, a part of me was dying inside too. I found myself looking after two households. Making meals and cleaning my parents' house was the only way I felt I could support my mother at the time. Having a clean home was so important to her, as she had cleaned other people's homes for a living. I was being an emotional support to my father and teaching *the farmer* how to do regular household chores. I thought it wouldn't be too big of task, and pretty straightforward, until he asked me, "Where does she keep the vacuum and how do I turn it on?" Between all these events happening and my finances dwindling faster than anticipated, you might say I was a ticking time bomb.

Within a year, virtually every support system I had was swept out from beneath my feet. Without my husband, my mother, and my community of friends for support, I was left to scrape myself up off the floor. I was bound and determined that I was going to take these experiences and rise above them. Thousands of dollars were spent on researching, reading books, taking courses, taking more courses, and then a few more. Every situation, every person I met, and every connection I made was an opportunity to change my circumstances. When I was open and willing, luck, fate, opportunity, divine intervention, karma, or whatever you want to call it, conveniently showed up. The exact, right people showed up at the right time, the message I needed to hear appeared, money started to flow towards me, and I began enjoying life.

So, how did I go from being overweight, broke, lonely, depressed, angry, stressed, and dreading getting out of bed in the morning, to feeling vibrant, slim, connected, happy, and grateful for everything in my life? I discovered and implemented the 5 Rs!

The 5 Rs for Long Lasting Change

There are three words that will take you out of the game before you even start. They are the most dangerous words you can say to yourself as you work towards growing yourself and reaching your goals. It has been said it takes at least seven times being exposed to a concept before you begin to truly understand it enough to apply the teachings. Commit to taking these three little words out of your vocabulary: *I know that.* As soon as your mind hears this, it automatically shuts off from being open to receive information, especially at a deeper level. Many times you *think* you know something, but if you are not applying what you know, you really don't know it. Does that make sense? So, stay open to learning, relearning, and learning in a new way. My mentors have taught me that if I am not doing something consistently, I don't understand the concept well enough yet. You may have been introduced to the 5 Rs that you will be learning about in this book. I strongly encourage you to refrain from telling yourself, "I know that," and losing the opportunity to grow.

There are five main requirements to changing your life easily and effectively. Without these foundational structures in place, trying to make changes will be stressful, challenging, and ultimately doomed from the start. The *5 Rs* of change I will be sharing with you in this book, will completely alter how you look

16

at making changes in your life, how you set goals for yourself, and what action steps you take to achieve those goals. If you ensure that all *5 Rs* are addressed, creating and manifesting the life you dream and desire will be quick, fun, and easy. Here is a quick overview of the 5 Rs before delving deeper into each one in the upcoming chapters.

Reason

The first step to achieving your dreams is discovering what it is YOU really want. This may appear to be simple and straightforward. Unfortunately, most people underestimate this groundwork and unknowingly set themselves up for failure before they even start out. Setting goals and intentions is more than just picking something to work on that is not going well in your life. If rocket ships are even a little off the target at the beginning of their journey, their trajectory will be increasingly off course, resulting in being nowhere near their goal at the end. This is the same for you! If you set out on a path for the wrong reasons, without the right supplies, or without a map of how to get there, the chances of reaching your destination is unlikely. Don't let this be your experience! In chapter 2, we will ensure you are heading out on the right path towards a destination that will be exactly what you were looking for, you will get the needed supplies required for your journey, and you will receive a map outlining the easiest and most fun way to get to your destination. How does it get better than that?! Let's face it, no one wants to get on a plane thinking they are headed to Hawaii and end up at the North Pole, especially when dressed for the beach.

Relationship

The second key component to creating change in your life is relationships. Think, together is better! No one achieved anything great by themselves. Contrary to popular opinion, asking for help does not mean you are incapable, weak, or stupid. Asking for support, and receiving support, is something that can feel difficult and awkward at first for a lot of people, but it does not have to feel that way. In Chapter 3, we will discuss how to do this in a way that is a win-win for everyone, as well as the importance of accountability buddies and what qualities are essential when choosing one. You will discover the importance of creating an atmosphere of positive, supportive groupies to surround yourself with, and renewing your relationship with yourself.

Relationships can be like the wind when you are flying a kite. Sure, you yourself can run and make things happen, but with just a little help from the right wind (support), your creation soars high, easily and effortlessly. The wrong type of wind or relationship, however, can destroy your kite, one pounding into the ground after another, despite your best efforts to take off.

Re-write

In this chapter, we will look at the science behind your mind and how to get your mind working for you instead of against you. This is the biggest change agent and the most important step to getting what you want. If your subconscious mind is not on board with what you are consciously thinking, you will experience all sorts of sabotage. A foundational concept that is key to making changes is: your thoughts create your emotions, and your emotions create your behaviours, and your behaviours equal your results. This means: What you think will determine how you feel, and how you feel will determine what you do. If you believe exercise is terrible and excruciating, you will feel unmotivated. When you feel unmotivated, it is very easy to hit the snooze button to miss a morning workout, or sit on the couch instead of going for a walk. Does that make sense? In Chapter 4, you will be given step by step tools and techniques that will support you in rewriting negative, unsupportive beliefs locked in your subconscious mind. You will learn how your mind works and how you can use it to make the changes you require in order to exceed your expectations for yourself. Changing just one thought or belief can cause a ripple effect to other areas of your life, allowing simultaneous success.

Repeat

Chapter 5 discusses the importance of creating repeating rituals and habits that are supportive and nurturing. This is not a religious practice, although it could be if that is important to you. Allowing time and space for an energetic renewal and connection is key, regardless of your spiritual beliefs. Reflecting on what is working and not working in your life allows you to adjust the course as needed. It forms an environment to focus on recognition of your successes so far, and gives you an opportunity to celebrate the progress you have made and recalibrate forward momentum. This chapter will provide you with specific exercises and tools to use in order to feel exactly how you want and need to feel every day to achieve your goals. You will learn how to be grateful for every bump in the road. Being able to shift into empowering, motivating, and uplifting energy, whenever it is required, makes the 'suck it up and do it days' a lot more enjoyable.

Rest and Rejuvenate

The final key component to change is rest and rejuvenation. For those of you that are extremely driven and used to being busy all the time, parts of this chapter may be challenging, or it may be that missing piece you needed. Often, we are so used to being 'on' that when it comes time to turn down the intensity, or shut off at the end of the day, we are too wound up. The results of not being able to relax can lead to dependency on sleeping pills, not getting enough sleep, turning to addictions, using distractions to avoid life, and being miserable. I have heard many people tell the story of finally taking a vacation after 51 weeks of stress, only to find they can't seem to relax or enjoy the down time. What is the point of working to reach a goal only to find you are too burned out to enjoy the accomplishment? Just as important as being able to power down and rest, your success also requires you to power up and become invigorated at times. There will be times on your path that you may lose momentum and drive. Knowing how to raise your energy, despite being unenthusiastic, is key to consistently taking steps forward. This chapter will assist you with practical ways to shift your energy to exactly where you need it to be.

These are the biggest and best change agents. So here we go! Get ready for the unimaginable transformation that will occur as you read the following pages and participate in the journey. Congratulations on saying yes to yourself and your dreams!

Homeplay: Ink Diarrhea

Time: 5-15+ minutes

Purpose: To become aware of your thoughts and be able to translate those thoughts onto paper. It will also serve as a base point of where you are now, and will be interesting to revisit when you are finished the book. When we write, especially with pen and paper instead of typing, we tap into different parts of our brain. Journaling, creative writing, ink diarrhea, or whatever you choose to call it, has been proven to be an effective form of becoming aware of thoughts and emotions, as well as releasing them. What you think, directly affects your level of success. Obviously, it is essential to become aware of what is going on in that head of yours, so you know what thoughts are blocking your efforts. Listen to that little voice in your head, as it is guiding your decisions.

Materials Required: Paper and Pen

Exercise:

Journal what you are thinking about after reading thus far and how you are feeling. The key to this is for you to let go of proper sentence structure, grammar, proper indentation, and all the etiquettes of writing you were taught in school. Yes, as a former high school English teacher, I give you permission to not use capitals and punctuation. Let the pen flow without thinking about or analyzing what you are writing. Don't worry if nothing comes to you—just keep writing. If you put your pen on the paper and all that comes to your mind is crickets chirping, write that down. *"I hear crickets chirping and I have no idea what to write."* Then, don't stop. Keep writing whatever comes to mind, even if it doesn't make sense or seem applicable. The little voice inside of you is always talking; it is just a matter of listening to that voice and keeping the pen moving. The more you practice this, the quantity and quality of your writing will improve. The more in depth you will go, the more you will surprise yourself and the more clarity you will find.

Important Note: Don't read what you wrote until you are completely finished.

I will give those of you, who are really struggling, some sentence starters to assist you in getting started. I recommend choosing only one, and then focusing on listening to the voice for what it has to tell you:

After reading thus far, I have come to realize...

The chapter I am most excited to read is...

When I read _____, I felt...

The thing I most want to change is... and this is why...

I feel...

Write a letter to yourself to read when you are finished the book.

Takeaway:

Reread what you wrote and pick out the key themes or feelings that show through. Begin to ask yourself questions such as: Was this exercise difficult or easy and why do you think so? Were the thoughts in my head mine or were they the words of someone else (i.e. parent or spouse)? How am I feeling moving forward? What is my take away from this exercise? Write down anything that comes up for you as you reflect on the exercise. You may find as you move through the book that similar themes show up, or you may use this piece of writing to see how far you have come by the time you are done reading.

Chapter 1: Key Concepts

- Change is only hard if you believe it to be.
- The outer world has a significant influence on our inner world.
- Identifying the lesson, gift, or take away from each experience is important; otherwise, it was a lost opportunity to create awareness and change.
- The body does what the mind tells it to.
- Thoughts -> feelings -> behaviours = results
- How you do one thing is how you do everything.
- You are worthy and deserving of your dreams; there are no pre-qualifications or requirements.
- Change is largely about changing our inner game to see the results in our outer world.
- The 5 Rs to change are Reason, Relationships, Re-Write, Repeat, and Rest and Rejuvenate.
- By writing down our thoughts, we can become aware of repeating patterns of thoughts and feelings.
- Awareness is the first step to change!

Chapter 2

Reason: Making it Real

This chapter is all about getting you set up and prepared to make your desires manifest as quickly and as easily as possible. Have you ever joined millions of people around the world to set New Year's resolutions? Have you ever been able to keep your resolution for the entire year? Statistically, only one out of ten people ever keep their New Year's resolutions past six months. That is only 10% of people are successful at what they set out to accomplish!

One of the reasons for low success rates is people are caught in what I call the Wishing Well Syndrome. They close their eyes and make a wish and hope the universe will magically make it come true. Obviously, this method will not get you the results you want. Wishing and dreaming have no action steps or guidelines on how you will actually achieve what you set out to do. There are many people who set weight loss goals this way. They decide, I want to be ___ pounds, or I want to lose ___ pounds. And that is it. They have no idea of how they will actually get there, but they have set the goal in their mind. If you are truly goal setting, there are specific action steps planned out and an end date in mind. Are you wish setting or are you goal setting?

Being the Captain of Your Life

In my two day live, Sail to Success Course, participants dive deep into the goal setting aspects of making their dreams a reality. This course is like the map and compass for your life. I will be sharing a few of the concepts in this book.

Where are you now? Determine where it is you currently are, so you can use the awareness to direct your course of action in the most efficient way possible. If we compare our lives to a sailboat in the ocean: Without certain criteria, we just aimlessly float around, hoping at some point to reach our destination, or remain sitting at shore, waiting for the island to come to us. We may dream of soft white sand and lush greenery, but, in reality, we are surrounded by none of this. How long does it take for us to give up on our goals, if we make no progress or see no results? In my experience, not very long! This is particularly true in the instant gratification culture we live in now.

There are five types of sailors, or people. Determine which of the following five sailor archetypes describe you the best:

1. Crying Maiden

Crying Maidens are the people on the sidelines or dock, upset that the ships have left without them. They were too scared to take action and are often stuck in indecision. These are the people that don't know what they want, how they would get it if they did figure it out, and don't want to risk stepping off the dock to try new things. You will spot these people quickly as they like to sit around and complain about how bad life and their situation is, but don't take any action to make their lives better. These are the people who sit on the sidelines, criticizing others for setting sail into the unknown and taking risks, while they don't usually achieve anything they really want. Crying Maidens are paralyzed by fear and avoid doing things outside the norm. The person in this archetype will typically be in a job or relationship they hate, for fear of leaving to something better. They will spend their days being miserable and are focused on negative possibilities of 'what if' this or that. I refer to these types of people as energy vampires. They suck the energy right out of you with their negative comments and outlook on life. Are you a Crying Maiden, or do you know someone who is?

2. Planks

Planks have read all the right books and are very knowledgeable. They have tools and know how to sail a ship or reach their goals, but they don't have the support of a crew. Can one person sail a big ship all by themselves? Possibly, when everything is going smoothly, but certainly not when storms or obstacles arise. These people start out strong, but find it too tough and daunting to get to their destination without help. Planks know what they need to do but don't have the support to take action effectively. The person in this archetype will often start working towards a goal but lose interest or quit before they are successful. Does this sound like you?

3. Mates

Unlike Planks, Mates people have a good crew or support network of family and friends. They are surrounded with people who cheer them on and will help them out. The problem is they have lots of support, but no one has any idea of what they are doing. It is the blind leading the blind, trying to sail a ship. They don't have the tools or knowledge to get them to their destination. This archetype will look like the person at a gym, lifting too much weight with improper form, surrounded by buddies encouraging him to do another rep. Another way it could show up is in a woman getting marriage advice from a friend who has never been in a long-term relationship. How far do you think these people will get? They will probably sink not far off shore.

4. Where's Waldo?

These people have the tools and knowledge of how to reach their goals, and they have a support group to help them out, but they are missing the third critical piece. They have no idea where they are going! They are making good time, to nowhere. These people are always busy and doing, but have little to show for their efforts, or are unfulfilled in their lives. They are achieving 'stuff' that is not what they truly desire. This archetype will often appear successful, but inside it can feel like something is missing or not quite right. Outsiders see a ship sailing gracefully with a well organized crew on deck, but what they don't realize is the ship is stopping at island after island, lost.

5. Captains

Captains have all three critical components to reach their goals: the tools and knowledge, support, and a clear vision of where they want to go. They arrive at their destinations quickly and smoothly and adjust for unforeseen circumstances and challenges that arise. They don't drift off course, or stop at obstacles, because they have a team helping them. People, who are the captains of their lives, feel free, fulfilled, and focused. They have great success in many areas of their life because they are in control of their thoughts, feelings, and actions.

Which type of sailor do you see yourself as right now? By the end of this book, you will have the ability to take the helm of your life and be the captain like you are supposed to be. In this chapter, the focus will be on the destination and the most efficient path to get there. You will discover what it is you really want, and how to set yourself up for success. Most importantly, you will discover how fun and enjoyable the journey can be to your goal!

Everyone wants to live on top of the mountain, but all the happiness and growth occurs while you're climbing it.
– Andy Rooney

Bringing Out the 4 Year Old

I am assuming, by reading this book, you want to make your life better in some way.

To make any change, it is first essential to examine WHY it is you want the change. Know your WHY! When your WHY is big enough, the HOW takes care of itself. Why? Why? Why? I invite you to bring out the curious 4 year old inside of you, to ask, "Why?"

Knowing your why, or the reason you want your goal, will support you in deciphering what your true desires are from those others have imposed upon you. Often, we think we want a certain goal, but the desire for the goal was originally someone else's thoughts or expectations placed upon us. This is often the case with a son taking over the family business, or going to university to study for the same career as his father. Is it really something he wanted, or is it someone else's vision? Another example is when women set the goal to lose weight. Often they want to lose weight because of someone else's idea of what beautiful looks like. There have been many stories of people who sacrifice everything to achieve their dreams, only to realize it is not what they thought it would be, or they are all alone at the top. What they thought they wanted is not really what they were looking for. It is like climbing a ladder to get to the top, only to realize the ladder is up against the wrong wall.

Avoid this, and make sure what you are aiming for is really something you are wanting. This book is about first finding out what you really want. I mean, at the core of your being, want. We are influenced, from the time we are aware of our surroundings to act and behave a certain way, to want and strive for certain things, and to accept or discredit particular ideas. Society, families, social groups, and even our environment, influence our decisions and guide our vision for our lives, whether we are aware of it or not. Do you want your goal for you, or is there another reason? Have you ever asked yourself, "What is the real reason I want my goal?"

Let's use Mary as an example. Mary's goal was to lose 30 pounds before a reunion she had the following summer. Is that what she really wants? No, it isn't. Why does she want to lose the 30 pounds? What she really wants is to feel confident, sexy, successful, and proud of herself. The 'losing 30 pounds' is one of the ways she can achieve that. It is the how, not the why. Does that make sense?

The why you want your goal will be a feeling you want from achieving the goal. There is a feeling desired behind every goal we set. Here are a few examples:

Goal: Start my own business

False Reasons Why:
To earn more money. Why do you want to earn more money?
To be my own boss. Why do you want to be your own boss?
To set my own hours. Why do you want to have flexible hours?

True Reasons Why:
To feel free, accomplished, successful, proud, and empowered.

Goal: Have a clean house

False Reasons Why:
In case someone comes over. Why do you want a clean house when you have guests?

<u>True Reasons Why</u>:
To feel in control, clear headed, comfortable, energetic, and refreshed.

<u>Goal</u>: Run a marathon

<u>False Reasons Why</u>:
To say I did it. What is the feeling you will have?

<u>True Reasons Why</u>:
To feel empowered, inspired, successful, expectant, and enlivened.

Homeplay: Why?

Time: 5-15+ minutes

Purpose: To get clarity about why you want your goal.

Materials Required: Paper and Pen

Exercise:

1. Choose any long-term goal that you would like to work towards. For this exercise, a long-term goal is considered a goal that will take over two months to achieve. This could be for any area of your life: physical, spiritual, intellectual, emotional, relationship, career, financial, social, family, etc. Write this goal down on a piece of paper.

2. Imagine, or pretend, that tomorrow morning, when you wake up, the goal you have set for yourself has come true. While you slept, all the work was done, and you now have achieved whatever it was you set out to achieve. Take a few moments to really imagine and get into the feeling of what it would feel like to have your goal realized. What might your body feel like once you achieved the goal? How would you feel? Make sure to feel the energy in your body of being successful.

3. Write down how you feel as though you have reached your goal. There is a list of feeling words at the back of this book to support you in getting specific in describing how you feel. You may also find it useful to search the internet for additional feeling words, or look up in a thesaurus similar words to get the exact words that resonate.

You may discover, when imagining reaching your goal, you feel negative feelings come up, or have difficulty getting excited for the outcome. This could show up as feelings of indifference, irritation, depression, isolation, deflation, etc. This is perfect feedback and awareness! Most often, feelings such as these suggest you do not really want the goal, or you are trying to achieve it for the wrong reasons. If this showed up for you, start this exercise again. This time, use a goal that is meaningful and something you are excited to work towards and achieve. If it is a goal you think you really want, journal about the goal to gain greater insight as to why you are having negative thoughts. Homeplay exercise: Ink Diarrhea from Chapter 1 can assist you in this process.

4. Write down as many words that feel applicable, then narrow it down to 3–5 words. This is what you are really wanting

from this goal. You can do this exercise with other goals as well. Look for similarities or patterns between the lists to help identify the main feelings you yearn to experience.

5. Write down this sentence and fill in the blank with the words that describe how you will feel when you achieve your goal.

What I really want from (insert your goal) is to feel (insert your 3–5 feeling words).

6. Instead of waiting one month, two months, six months, or a year to feel how you want to feel by achieving your goal, why not start feeling that way now? Ask yourself, "How can I feel (insert 3–5 feeling words you came up with) now?"

For example:

What I really want from *losing 30 pounds* is to feel *sexy, confident, and successful.*

I can feel *sexy* by: styling my hair nicely, wearing perfume, wearing sexy underwear, putting on a dress or skirt instead of pants, switching my sneakers for high heels, etc.

I can feel confident by: looking people in the eyes when I am talking to them, standing tall with good posture, wearing clothes that I feel good in, exercising, etc.

I can feel successful by: doing what I say I am going to do, focusing on what is important to me, making a list of all my accomplishments, writing down five things I was successful at every day, etc.

7. Post your goal, and how you want to feel, somewhere that you can see it every day. Ideal places are your bathroom mirror, a bedside table, or by your computer screen. This will serve as a reminder to take little action steps of being in the energy of how you want to feel. I will be discussing this in greater detail later on, but, for now, just do something every day to get yourself feeling how you want to feel when you achieve your goal.

Takeaway:

Shifting the focus to how you want to feel will make taking action steps towards your goal easier, and you will achieve your desired results quicker. When focusing on the desired feelings, it is not necessary to create new goals and add tasks to your list. Small simple shifts in the choices you make throughout your day will make a monumental impact. Know that you are worthy and deserving to feel the way you want to feel!

If you correct your mind,
the rest of your life will fall into place.
– Lao Tzu

Passionate and Sexy

You want your goal to be just like your man: big, realistic, strong, true, fun, passionate, and sexy. No one wants to spend time and effort sacrificing for mediocrity. Time is our most valuable asset, so avoid wasting it on tasks and goals that are not going to give you a big payoff in the end. Spend your valuable time doing what you love and what gives you the biggest rewards!

What if you don't know what it is you are passionate about? There are a hundreds of resources, tests, questionnaires, courses, and books created to help you find your life purpose and passion. Begin with the end in mind. If you want to end up feeling happy, successful, and accomplished, then start with goals working towards creating these feelings in your life. Use the feeling words at the back of this book to support you in finding which words fit for you. It can be as simple as thinking of your favourite scene in a movie, or favourite part of a book, and asking what feeling was the character embracing? What was happening in movies, books, poems, or in real life, that gave you goosebumps? Be curious and open, and trust that whatever feeling words you arrive at are the perfect ones for you now.

Once you know how you want to feel, brainstorm some outcomes that could create that for you. If you want to feel confident, for example, who do you know who does something, that when you see them, you feel their confidence? What activities create feelings of confidence for you? Another way to expand your brainstorm list is to do research on the internet. You can combine feelings to narrow it down even more. When you know how you want to feel, the paths to getting there are endless. It is simply a matter of choosing one path and setting a goal to get there.

When we decide to set a goal, how we set a goal is just as important as why we set the goal or intention. Goals must be stated in a positive way. Our brains, particularly under stress, will not register the word NOT. An example of this is setting the goal of, "I will not spend money when I go to the mall today." Our mind processes that as, "I will spend money when I go to the mall today." It ignores the word NOT, giving you the exact opposite of what you were wanting— spending money! I sense that there are a few lightbulbs going on with readers of this book right now. If you focus on what you don't want, you will get more of that. What you focus on expands! Have you ever noticed, the minute you set a goal, obstacles that were never a problem before start showing up? For me, this happened when I set the goal to stop eating junk food. I never had a big sweet tooth, but give me a bag of salt 'n vinegar chips, and my tongue would be sore for a week afterwards. Because I was focused on the words junk food, I began craving chocolate, which was something I never really enjoyed before! Do you see what I am saying? If I had set the goal to "eat only healthy foods," my mind would have focused on healthy foods, resulting in a different experience. Your goals need to be passionate and sexy, not fear and anxiety producing! Who wants to stop, quit, or not do something they previously enjoyed? Nobody.

In addition to this, we want goals to have a deadline of when we are planning on accomplishing it; otherwise, it will turn into a 'someday goal.' You have heard people, maybe even yourself, say, "I am going to do such and such...someday." So, when will you actually start to take action steps, if you are going to do it 'someday?' Sure, it is something you say you want to achieve, but 'someday' is not a day of the week on your calendar. Meaning, someday is equal to no day. Some people are resistant to putting an actual date down for fear of not accomplishing their goal by that time. The brain operates in clear, concrete messages. If you have no deadline, it will interpret that to mean 'someday.' You will then be stuck in wish setting, not goal setting.

Having a deadline drives motivation and keeps you on track. How will you know if you have arrived at your destination? How will you know you have achieved your goal? Your goal must be clear and specific enough that you will know if you have achieved it. For example, I want to be rich could be something you are aiming for. What is rich? For one person, it could mean having food on the table and a roof over their head, while to someone else it means having millions of dollars in their bank account. The brain measures in clear, concrete messages and does not understand vague, unclear statements that are up for interpretation. The goal, I will earn one hundred thousand dollars next year, is not wishy washy or abstract. The mind can comprehend this clarity and begin supporting you.

Another aspect of a properly formed goal is for it to be stated in a powerful tense, using I will, or I have, or, most powerful, I choose to. For example, the goal of "I want to lose weight" is not a good goal for a couple of reasons. One, it is not specific. How much weight? Is it just about the scale number or are there other ways to measure your success? Reason two, it keeps you in a state of wanting. Stating, "I want..." keeps you in a state of never having what it is you want. The goal is to 'want,' so congratulations, you are already successful! You already achieved wanting to lose weight.

As an aside, for those of you who have weight loss as a goal, there is a small shift in the way you say your goal to make it easier for your brain to assist in making it a reality. What happens when you lose our keys? Your brain automatically begins to go searching looking for them. This is the same thing that happens when you say you want to lose weight. Your brain thinks you have lost something, a typically undesirable event, so it does everything to find the weight again. This shows up as sabotaging behaviours, losing weight only to find it again (a.k.a. yo-yo dieting), not being able to lose weight, etc. Instead of saying you want to 'lose' weight, reframe that into releasing weight. Releasing something suggests to your brain that it is something you desire and it is safe to do. Your brain's job is to keep you safe, so if it interprets losing something as a threat, seeing the numbers go down on the scale will be a struggle.

One of the most common causes of failure is the habit of quitting when one is overtaken by temporary defeat.
– Napoleon Hill

Homeplay: NOT!

Time: 5-10+ minutes

Purpose: To reframe your goal into clear and concrete statements of what you want vs what you don't want, have a date to accomplish your goal, and state it in the powerful tense.

Materials Required: Paper and Pen

Exercise:

1. What are the top three negatively framed goals you say to yourself? Write these down on a piece of paper, e.g., I want to stop yelling at my kids.

2. Next, reframe these goals into the positive without using the word NOT or NO. For those of you who are a bit rebellious and creative, words that are contractions for NOT (can't, don't, etc.), or the words stop, quit, and never, are also forbidden. Think—What do I want vs. what don't I want, e.g., I want to speak calmly to my children vs. I want to stop yelling at my kids.

3. Ensure your goal uses the powerful tense, I will, or I have, but, preferably, I choose to, e.g., I choose to speak calmly to my children.

4. Make sure your goal is specific enough that you will know when you have achieved it. You can actually measure your success on some type of scale, e.g., I choose to speak calmly to my children five out of seven days of the week.

5. Set a date to complete this goal by, e.g., I choose to speak calmly to my children five out of seven days of the week, by September 15th of this year.

Takeaway:

Can you feel the excitement rising in your body? Framing what you want instead of what you don't want is more powerful and will get you the results you are looking for. Being specific and clear on what it is that you are aiming for, assists your brain in finding ways to the paths of least resistance in order to create success. It operates and responds best from clear and concrete messages. This exercise can be done for short and long-term goals. Keep your goal around you and read it several times a day, because what you focus on, expands! Where attention goes, energy flows!

Stop Chasing the Rainbow

How many people do you know who start out enthusiastic about a goal, only to quit a few weeks, or even days, afterwards? Is this something you tend to do? Focusing on the end result, or the long-term goal, can be empowering, but, often, it can also result in feelings of inadequacy, defeat, and overwhelm. It reminds us of how far we have to go before being successful. The goal is too far away to feel like we can achieve it.

Metaphorically, we are standing at A in the alphabet and realizing there are a whole lot of steps and time commitment involved before we get to Z. This chapter is about shifting your perspective and main focus from Z to the next letter down the line from where you are right now—essentially, looking at the next step required instead of all the steps required. Small tasks and action steps are easier to take, and less overwhelming, than just focusing on the ever-elusive pot of gold at the end of the rainbow. Goal setting has to be about enjoying the journey, not just the destination.

People who run long distances races, such as marathons, don't focus on the finish line. They focus on the next landmark, the next turn, the next mile. This is how the mindset of a goal setter needs to be. If marathon runners obsessed on how they have 18 miles left to go, very few participants would finish the race. Know that your final destination is Z, but focus primarily on the next step, or group of steps, coming up. This supports in keeping motivation levels high. A small task completed gives a sense of accomplishment. Accomplishment leads to motivation and action. Small gains repeated equal large rewards.

Chunking goals down into year, month, week, and day action steps makes the goal feel achievable and concrete, as opposed to far off and abstract. I know if my goal was to run a marathon by the end of the year, and if I focused on the 26 miles, I would be quitting before I even started. However, if we break the seemingly overwhelming task into manageable parts, we have the inspiration and motivation to take action. The following is an example of chunking down goals:

1 Year Goal: Complete a 26 mile marathon
9 Month Goal: Run/walk 26 miles without stopping
6 Month Goal: Be able to run 13 miles without stopping
5 Month Goal: Be able to walk/run 10 miles without stopping
4 Month Goal: Be able to run 8 miles without stopping
3 Month Goal: Be able to run 5 miles without stopping
2 Month Goal: Be able to run 2.5 miles without stopping
1 Month Goal: Be able to run 1 mile without stopping
3 week Goal: Be able to run 0.5 miles without stopping
2 week Goal: Be able to run/walk 1 mile
1 week Goal: Be able to walk 1 mile
Tomorrow's Goal: Walk 0.5 miles
Today's Goal: Walk around the block

This is just a simple example of how someone could chunk down the one year goal of completing a marathon. For your goals, you will want to be more detailed and have many more action steps within each section: like increasing the amount of water you drink, eating a diet that is most appropriate for athletes who are training, getting a running buddy or coach, researching how to avoid injuries while training, etc. Is this the plan everyone should follow who wants to run a marathon? No, of course not! It depends on where you are starting at physically, and other factors that come into play. Before embarking on any physical goal, I highly recommend having a check up with your local physician. This example is merely to demonstrate the technique of chunking.

Starting today, if all you needed to do was walk around the block, does that seem doable for most people? Sure! Start at A and look at the next small step to B. Once you are at B, look at C next. Small steps of success build momentum and increase the dopamine in your brain. Dopamine is a neurotransmitter in your brain that enables you to take action towards your visions, and resist impulses and temptations. People with low levels of dopamine are more likely to have self harming habits such as addictions because it is in charge of our pleasure/reward system. High dopamine leads to high motivation, which leads to a high rate of success. As important as focusing on the here and now is, it is also important that you look up every once in awhile to make sure you are still on track and headed towards the goal you started on. You only need to look at Z, or your end goal, long enough to make sure all the letters and steps on the path still lead you to your desired outcome.

Before you start chunking your long-term goals, there is an important distinction between performance goals and outcome goals you must become aware of.

Outcome goals focus on achieving a certain result or outcome that is out of our control. A good example of this is someone wanting to lose 30 pounds. Setting the goal of losing two pounds every week seems realistic, but as anyone who has ever tried to lose weight knows, it is not how weight loss works in reality. When dieters are not able to achieve the result they want, they get discouraged and will often quit before reaching their goal.

Performance goals, however, are focused on behaviour and actions that are easy to assess rather than focusing just on the result or outcome. This gives a sense of control and empowerment. With empowerment comes motivation and dedication, making it easier to achieve success. An example of a performance goal is walking 45 minutes every day, five times a week. Can achieving this type of goal get you a result of losing 30 pounds? Sure! The focus is on the action step, not on the result.

Another example of performance vs outcome goals could be a salesman wanting to increase his income. An outcome goal he could set is earning $100,000 next year. The problem is, he has no control over whether he makes that much money. He does, however, have control over the actions he takes, like making 10 cold calls per week, increasing his advertising and marketing, taking sales trainings, etc. With each successful action step, his motivation rises, thus encouraging him to persevere.

Performance goals are more empowering and in your control. Focus on what you can control for motivation and forward momentum.

Your turn!

Homeplay: Ready, Set, Chunk!

Time: 15-45+ minutes

Purpose: To chunk long-term outcome goals into smaller, manageable performance goals and action steps. This will support in creating the thoughts and feelings of your goal being achievable and reachable. It is also to purposely plan action steps to feeling how you want to feel along the way, rather than waiting until the end to get the feelings you desire.

Materials Required: Paper and Pen

Exercise:

1. Choose a long-term goal that is at least six months away from being achieved. It must be an emotionally powerful goal, meaning you get emotional at the thought of achieving it, e.g., goosebumps, rush of adrenaline, tears come to your eyes, etc.

2. List the months, working backwards from your end goal. These will serve as stepping stones to get to the finish line.

3. For the last month: list week three, week two, and week one goals.

4. For the first week: list each day, so you can write an action step(s) for those days.

5. Chunk down time! Begin planning steps to reach your goal. It does not matter if they are the 'perfect' steps or the absolute 'right' steps. Over the six months or year, you will need

to readjust, depending on your progress and learnings along the way, e.g., at five months you may get an injury setting you back, or you may be achieving success faster than you thought possible. Planning it out now, gives you a map and guideline of where you need to be approximately in relation to your goal at a particular point in time along the path. Be sure to include action steps that will create the feelings you want to have when you arrive at your end goal. If you are unsure of what these feelings are, refer back to the exercise, Homeplay: Why? from earlier in this chapter. Without a plan, you don't know where you are going, how you will get there, or where you will end up. This is the most important and most overlooked step to achieving your desires and dreams.

Remember to start small and attainable working your way up! Some people find it easier to plan from the six month mark and work their way back to the present day, and others prefer to start at the present day and plan their way forward to the six months mark. Whichever way works for you, is perfect!

Takeaway:

Planning small manageable steps along the path to your goal is key to success. Including goals along the way that create the feelings you desire from achieving your goal, generates momentum and perseverance. Focus on performance goals versus outcome goals, so you feel more in control and motivated. The steps you thought you originally were required to take may change as you go along. Be open and flexible to adjust your course as new information and self discoveries occur. Accept that you may not be able to see the exact path you need to take to get you to the finish line from the start line, however, without a plan, you will not be able to take effective action.

> *If you don't know where you are going,*
> *any road will get you there.*
> – Lewis Carroll

Homeplay: Fear Brainstorming

Time: 15-30+ minutes

Purpose: To become aware of underlying fears or considerations, and brainstorm possible solutions.

Materials Required: Paper and Pen

Exercise:

Create a chart with two columns. On the left hand side, list ten fears or considerations you have when thinking about taking the steps required to achieving your goal, or actually achieving your goal. On the right hand side of the table, brainstorm as many solutions to that fear or consideration as possible. Whatever wild and crazy thoughts come to your head, write them down. Do not edit as you go! If you feel stuck, ask a friend for ideas. The following is a condensed example from a client who wanted to release weight.

Fear	Solutions
Being hungry if I eat less	-eat slower so I know when I am full -drink more water -focus on my food and eating instead of watching television -go to bed earlier instead of being tempted to eat late at night -eat snacks between meals instead of three big meals -eat vegetables instead of junk food when I want to eat
If I don't eat lots then I won't be getting my money's worth at buffets	-stop eating at buffets -write my goal on a piece of paper and have it in front of me when I'm eating -eat mainly vegetables -limit myself to one plate
People will be staring at me when I go to the gym	-hire a body guard to give intimidating stares to anyone who looks my way -bring barriers to put around me while I workout -say 'what are you staring at' to anyone who looks at me -buy equipment to exercise at home -go to the gym with a friend -exercise outside -say positive affirmations to myself when I am there

Takeaway:

Creating solutions to fears beforehand helps to minimize the fear. Fear is the biggest obstacle to overcome in your quest for change. This exercise is like preparing a preemptive strike against your critical and sabotaging thoughts. You have a specific plan in place for when that fear shows up. Planning and preparing is one of the best solutions to combat fear and sabotage.

Stop being afraid of what could go wrong, and start being excited of what could go right.
— Tony Robbins

Chapter 2: Key Concepts

- When your WHY is big enough, the HOW takes care of itself.
- Working towards a goal, without being clear on why you want that goal, is like climbing to the top of a ladder, only to find out it is up against the wrong wall.
- There is a feeling desired behind every goal we set.
- The WHY you want your goal will be a feeling you are wanting from achieving the goal.
- Time is our most valuable asset, so spend it doing what you love.
- Goals must be stated in a positive way. Our brains, particularly under stress, will not register the word NOT.
- What you focus on expands!
- Someday is not a day of the week on your calendar. Setting a goal to be completed someday is wish setting, not goal setting.
- Your goal must be clear and specific enough that you will know if you have achieved it.
- A properly formed goal is for it to be stated in a powerful tense using I will, or I have, or I choose to.
- Our brain's job is to keep us safe.
- Framing what you want instead of what you don't want is more powerful and will get you the results you are looking for.
- Where attention goes, energy flows!
- Goal setting has to be about enjoying the journey, not just the destination.
- Small gains repeated equal large rewards.
- Focus on performance goals rather than outcome goals, as performance goals are in your control.

- Focus on what you can control for motivation and forward momentum.
- Creating solutions to fears beforehand helps to minimize the fear.

Chapter 3

Relationship: Together is Better

The word relationship in its simplest form means the state of being connected. Connection includes relationship with ourselves, with others, with nature, and with a higher power. When our life here on earth is coming to an end, we want to be surrounded by, and be connected to, the people who love us. I have yet to know of anyone to want fancy clothes, cars, or toys to be their comforting exit.

Why is that? Connection is what brings fulfillment, meaning, and purpose to our lives. Maslow's hierarchy of needs states that after our physiological and safety needs are met, love and belonging is the next step in our growth and evolution. Being in healthy connection with others has been proven to improve our quality and longevity of life. How can having good quality relationships support you in achieving your goals? That is what this chapter is all about! We will look at improving the relationship with yourself, surrounding yourself with a strong support network, and creating boundaries that both protect you and strengthen the connection while in relation to others.

I wish I didn't have so many
good relationships and connections.
– said no one ever.

Look Me in the Eyes and Tell Me You Love Me

Would you say you have a good relationship with yourself? Most of us think we do because, for the most part, we know what we like or don't like, about our past and our deepest secrets. But, do you respect yourself? Do you love yourself? Would you do anything for you? Are you at the top of your priority list? At the surface, most people answer yes.

Unfortunately, it takes little time to look around at society and realize that we are not cherishing ourselves, respecting ourselves, and treating our bodies as sacred. The abuse of alcohol, drugs, sedentary lifestyles, junk foods, over eating, under eating, etc., is rampant. These are all forms of self punishment, self hate, and disrespect.

If you don't love yourself, no one else can truly love you. You won't let them. You will block them out, resist, sabotage, defend, and even attack others, to protect yourself. Do you behave and act differently around different groups of people? Do you show up as the same person at work as you do at family gatherings? Most people don't because they feel that they are not good enough, not smart enough, not beautiful enough, not funny enough, not talented enough, not successful enough, etc. They create personas and wear masks to present themselves a certain way with the intent to be accepted. Without this persona, they think they will not be accepted or liked. What if you showed up as your authentic self all the time? What if you didn't have to pretend to be someone else so people would like you? What if people actually liked and respected you more for being authentically you? From my experience, people can easily detect others who are putting on a show or feeding them B.S.

Loving yourself starts with accepting who you are—loving your shiny, likeable parts and the dark shadow parts you try not to show others. Everyone has a dark shadow side. The more we try to disconnect with our shadow selves, the more it takes over and presents itself, to let you know it is still there. It is like trying to hold a beach ball (the parts we don't want people to see) under water. How much energy does that take? A lot!!! When you try to be everything to everybody, you end up being nothing to nobody. Let go of the shields, the masks, the personas, and be willing to be vulnerable and raw to let your brightest light shine. When grounded completely in who you are and what you believe in, you won't be thrown off track by others' opinions, shiny objects, or society and family pressures. After all, most people go around thinking they are giving helpful advice when they are acting more like porcupines: a lot of fine points, but not much for meat. Being able to listen to the voice inside that is your true self, or your higher self, instead of the monkey chatter in your head, will assist you in making clearer choices. Clearer choices makes progress faster. It all starts with loving and accepting yourself.

Nothing binds you except your thoughts; nothing limits you except your fear; and nothing controls you except your beliefs.
– Marianne Williamson

Homeplay: Mirror Mirror

Time: 1 minute every day

Purpose: To change the negative beliefs about yourself into love and acceptance.

Materials Required: Mirror

Exercise:

Stand in front of a mirror. Say the following words out loud to yourself while you look yourself in the eye: "I love and approve of myself." This specific affirmation is from Louise Hay's book, *You Can Heal Your Life,* which I highly recommend. Keep repeating the words and let them sink in deep. Feel their impact and notice what body sensations or thoughts arise. If you have issues with body image, an extra challenge is to do this exercise naked.

Note: If you have negative thoughts arise, simply say, "Thank you for sharing," and then repeat, "I love and approve of myself." Acknowledging the negative chatter, but not accepting it, gives you power and control. I like to think of it as a 3 year old trying to get my attention. If I just ignore the toddler, he will continue to repeat, "Mom, Mom, Mom...," until he feels heard. The same goes for that pesky monkey chatter that goes against something you believe to be true. The negative thoughts that can show up during this Homeplay exercise are nothing more than unsupportive beliefs you are carrying. Beliefs, as will be discuss further in chapter 4, are just made up stories that can be rewritten.

Takeaway:

We have been taught since we were little not to accept ourselves for who we are, through advertisements, social pressures, wanting to fit in and be accepted, and a variety of other ways. Most people, when starting this exercise, have some form of negative reaction, whether that be a cringe, an unsupportive thought, or a tightening in their stomach. This is simply feedback that this is unfamiliar, and that you probably have a belief that you don't deserve love, aren't worthy of it, don't want to look conceited, aren't good enough, or have a variety of other self defeating thoughts. Are these types of beliefs serving you? Of course not!

The more you practice this exercise, the easier it becomes, and the quicker you will see the ripple effect of an increasing amount of supporting, empowering thoughts. When a person loves and approves of themselves, they attract positive and loving energy into their lives. Life gets easier because others opinions do not matter, and you are no longer allowing your precious energy to get sucked away. You are able to stay focused on what is most important to you because you are your highest priority.

My children are my greatest teachers and mirrors for what I am projecting out into the world. After my divorce, I began dating a short six years later. (I spent a lot of time working on myself and learning how to not repeat the past.) When I first introduced my children to my boyfriend's family, I wanted to make a good impression and had some old programming from my childhood running. I was putting pressure on myself to have the perfect children who were seen but not heard, and followed any directions I gave them without complaint. Everything was going well, and my son was off playing with the other children. I was relieved that everyone was getting along and began to relax. It was about this time when my then six year old came up to the table of adults, who were sitting visiting, and pronounced very loudly, "I just love myself soooooo much!" He gave himself a big hug, then ran off to continue playing. Initially, I was embarrassed because everyone began to laugh, but the embarrassment quickly transformed to overwhelming joy and gratitude. I could feel his deep sense of self-acceptance and pride in acknowledging just how amazing he really is. That was one of my proudest moments as a mother, so far. If I can teach my children how to love and respect themselves, put themselves as the number one priority in their own lives, be compassionate, loving and giving to others, and be caring contributing members of society, I will have succeeded as a mother.

Children are like little sponges that suck up everything we do, so make sure what they are taking in and internalizing is positive and supportive to their growth and evolution. Although it can feel like a triumph somedays just to get them to follow directions, we are not raising robots. We don't want children to simply respond and follow our commands, but to critically analyze, problem solve, be internally driven, and have a love for themselves and those around them.

Let's raise children who won't have to
recover from their childhoods.
– Pam Leo

The Story That Changed My Life

Having great relationships starts with the relationship with yourself. Now, I didn't believe this for a large part of my life. As a result, I had a lot of relationships, although not many fulfilling ones. I was a people pleaser and a giver. I would give and give and give, and when I didn't have anything left, I would become resentful and point my fingers at that person, blaming them for my unhappiness. This concept slapped me in my face during my marriage. I put my kids first, my husband second, my work third, and, eventually, my needs were somewhere near the bottom of the list. It wasn't until after my divorce that I realized if I don't look after myself first, I can't help anyone. If my metaphorical gas tank is empty, this vehicle is not serving a purpose. No one could fill me up, no one could do the work for me, and no one could love me the way I wanted to be loved because I didn't even love myself. How could I truly allow someone else to love me, if I didn't even think I deserved to be at the top of my own priority list?!

Putting yourself as number one on the priority list reminds me of a pre-flight safety demonstration. When flying in an airplane, the message is always to put your own oxygen mask on first before assisting others. Why do you think this is?

You will not be able to help others if you haven't taken care of yourself first. You will literally run out of oxygen. If you don't choose you before others, you are doing those people in your life a disservice. Think of the mother who always puts her family before her own needs. She is often miserable, resentful, moody, tired, depressed, and worn out. Is she truly helping her family by putting herself last on the list?

57

Deciding that you are important enough to get your needs met, actually supports those around you that you care about. The mother that turns her life around by exercising every day, and eating healthy meals, role models these behaviours to her children. Your family needs you to be at your best! So choose not to feel guilty about taking time away for you to nurture yourself: exercise, have a relaxing bubble bath, a weekend away with friends, or whatever it is that you choose to do to love yourself. You (and your family) will be happier, have more energy, and feel more connected. I guarantee it!

As soon as you see yourself as worthy and deserving of your goals, the path to success will be smoother and more enjoyable. When you value yourself, carving out time to fulfill your own needs and desires becomes automatic, almost like a reflex. One of the biggest excuses I hear on why people don't reach their goals is they "don't have the time." We all have the same amount of hours in a day, the only difference is what we choose to do with our time. Choosing to numb out to television, commit to obligations that aren't in alignment with what you want, saying yes when you really want to say no, or being prideful and not asking for support, puts you at the bottom of the list. If you use the "I don't have time," or some version of the "when things slow down" excuse, stop torturing yourself with lies. The truth is, if you can't find time right now to permanent marker your needs to the top of the list, there will never be a good time. You will forever be under the illusion that it will happen when things change, when this project ends, when this gets done, etc. There is no better reason and no excuse big enough that trumps self-love. At the core of who you are is a desire to help others and offer your gifts to the world. Fulfilling your core desires takes treating yourself as though you were precious. It takes treating your body, mind, and spirit as powerful, influential, and valuable. It takes putting your needs first.

Do you treat yourself as though you are the most important person? Or is there always someone else's needs, wants, and dreams that come before yours? People do not like you for what you do for them; they love you for how you make them feel. By loving and valuing yourself, you give others permission to do the same. Help others by helping yourself first.

You have been criticizing yourself for years and it hasn't worked. Try approving of yourself and see what happens.
– Louise Hay

Homeplay: Oxygen Mask

Time: 5 minutes–An Entire Day

Purpose: To have a variety of ways to love yourself and make it easy to put yourself first on your priority list.

Materials Required: Paper and Pen

Exercise:

Brainstorm as many ways as you can (min. 100) to show love, acceptance, respect, and appreciation for who you are. It may help to make categories to narrow down and expand on certain areas. Areas that you can show love, acceptance, respect, and appreciation to yourself could include: physical, emotional, spiritual, intellectual, financial, career/job, things that cost money, things that are free, things I can do every day, ways to celebrate me, hobbies I enjoy, ways to relax, ways to nurture myself (without the use of food), boundaries I need to set, relationships I want to create/recreate/dissolve, etc.

Here is a short list of examples to get your mind flowing:

Physical – eating a variety of fruits and vegetables, drinking adequate amounts of water, moving your body at least 30 minutes every day, stretch, getting regular medical checkups, protecting your skin from damaging sun rays, etc.

Emotional – forgive others and yourself, do what you say, don't play small (meaning living your passion and purpose), saying positive affirmations, meditating, journaling, taking personal development classes, saying no to obligations that are not fulfiling, etc.

Ways to celebrate me – have a party, spend an entire day in nature, go for a walk, get a boudoir photoshoot, sign up for a pole dancing class, sleep in, go to the spa, read a book, splurge on an item I wouldn't ordinarily buy (if debt is a problem avoid this one), watch a funny movie, sign up for a class, make a scrapbook of my life, go on a vacation, etc.

My Challenge to you:

You love others by doing things for them, spending quality time with them, saying positive and caring messages, buying them gifts, and giving them hugs. How do you love yourself? Do you spend quality time alone with yourself? Do you say positive affirmations to yourself or that you love yourself? Do you treat yourself to gifts because you are special?

If you are like most people, you spend a majority of your time focused on pleasing and tending to others and very little time caring for yourself. I challenge you, if you are willing, to commit to yourself that you will consciously take at least one loving action each day just for YOU, for the next 21 days. This could be as quick and simple as looking in the mirror and giving yourself a compliment and telling yourself that you are worthy and deserving. Or you could do something extravagant like go on a trip or buy yourself something special that you always wanted. Whatever it is that you choose, the challenge is for you to feel loved and cared for, by you, in a conscious way, at least once per day.

Of course, as this becomes easier, move to twice a day, and so forth.

Takeaway:

Taking loving actions for yourself creates a journey through life that is enjoyable and relaxing. Instead of strenuously striving towards goals, glide with love. Many women, particularly mothers, struggle with putting themselves first or finding time to put themselves on the calendar at all. This will most likely require you to say no to others. This is not selfish! Burning out and creating overwhelm for yourself is not helping you or your family, it puts additional stress and tension on the relationships. When I first started practicing putting myself first, I simply explained to my children that this is 'mommy time,' and that mommy needs her alone time, so I can be a better mom. At first, I had all the negative thoughts and past programming of: "I am a bad mother not giving my children attention; your children are supposed to be number one; I am being selfish; I am not as important as my children." This can be especially difficult if your children are very young and do need immediate attention frequently. Brainstorm ways to get them involved with you to do self care. Often, I had my children exercise with me. They loved waiting for a high five at the top of my sit-ups, or sitting on my back while I did pushups. Eventually, they were beside me trying to mimic my actions and still do years later. We had spa days at home where we would take turns pampering each other, painting fingernails, giving back massages, or playing hairdresser. My children now recognize in themselves when they need to respect their limits and take time for themselves. Teach others to put their own oxygen masks on first by being a role model yourself.

Hula Hoop of Heaven

At the beginning of this book, I gave the analogy of your life being like a ship.

This part of the chapter will provide you with the guidelines of why you need, and how you get, a crew of people around you that are going to help you set sail. You will learn to quickly decipher if the people you are in conversation with have what it takes, or will drag you down and drown you. Discovering how easy it can be to let go of the need to do everything on your own can be a game changer for many people.

Creating a support network and surrounding yourself with like-minded people is key to achieving any goal. Not just anyone can fulfill this duty. Would you want just anyone off the street to come help you sail a ship? I don't think so! You are in search of people determined to expedite your growth and evolution and keep you committed and accountable. Everyone knows that two heads are better than one. What if you had eight or ten heads? How small would your obstacles become if you had a team of people supporting you, leading you, and cheering you on?

Deliberately seek the company of people who influence you to think and act on building the life you desire.
– Napoleon Hill

We become our environment. Have you ever noticed this? When we surround ourselves with positive uplifting people, our energy and thoughts become more positive. It is easy to believe in ourselves and our visions if someone else is dreaming big too.

What about spending time with negative, depressing people? Sure, it can bring your energy down. These energy vampires are the people from whom you can actually feel the life force energy being sucked right out of you. They are like Eeyore from Winnie the Pooh—Woe is me, everyone is out to get me, nothing goes my way, if I didn't have bad luck I wouldn't have any luck at all, etc. They play the role of victim for a majority of their life. Do you have energy vampires in your life? Are you yourself an energy vampire?

You will know you are with these people when they point out all the obstacles in your way, give you reasons why it isn't possible, how you aren't good enough, smart enough, or rich enough to do whatever it is you dream of. They are the people who are afraid to take risks and go out of their own comfort zone. They let fear run their lives and are dedicated to making sure everyone else stays in the uncomfortable comfort zone.

Many people have that one friend in their lives that is their crab friend. The person they call first to complain, gossip, and crab to. What happens during these conversations? Each person starts trying to up the other person with how bad they have it and what is going wrong in their lives. There is no problem solving or observational analyses, only focusing on how bad the situation is. People stuck in this rut feel unfulfilled and unhappy a majority of the time. They are comfortable being uncomfortable. Surround yourself with positive people, however, and you will achieve your goals much quicker and feel good about yourself along the way. The power of positive people pays off.

We can surround ourselves with people who are positive, but that alone is not going to get us to our goal. To have a quality support network, the people must have a common goal or commonality between them. Spending time with people who have similar goals and dreams will feed your motivation and drive, because you can learn from one another and support each other. Have you ever been faced with a situation that no matter how many times you turned it over in your mind, you just couldn't find a solution? What did you do next? You probably reached out and phoned a friend or business partner to ask their advice. Sometimes a new perspective or someone with a different experience level can offer options that were not even considered beforehand. What if you had a group of people working together to come up with ways to make your journey easier, faster, and more fun? What if, when obstacles arose, you had a team helping you over the wall and celebrating with you when you overcame diversity? For many, this is the missing piece to their success.

Let's use an analogy to make this a bit clearer. Could you go out and run a marathon right now? I am going to assume most people would not be able to accomplish this. Some of you may be thinking that it could never happen. But, what if you had two years with a personal trainer who specializes in training marathon runners? Could you run a marathon then? Possibly. The chances you could do this increased slightly, right? What if you had a personal trainer, personal nutrition chef, full time mindset coach, babysitters if needed, a paid two year leave from your job, with a $2 million reward just for finishing the race? Many of you are probably wondering where to sign up.

This is simply to demonstrate that you can accomplish anything with the right tools, the right coaches, the right incentives, the right support network, and the right perspective. The goal may seem out of reach or difficult to reach from where you are standing, but having a team of support helping lift you up and over the obstacles standing in your way is immeasurable.

Chapter 7: Perfectly Imperfect goes into specific detail of how to create a successful network of likeminded people. Being the captain of your ship and your life requires mates to assist, support, and inspire. Don't underestimate the importance of setting up a strong network and crew to make your goals a reality.

Environment is stronger than willpower.
– Buckminster Fuller

Accountability

In addition to having a group of like-minded people, you will also require more individual one on one support, such as an accountability buddy. An accountability buddy is someone who does just what the name implies—keeps you accountable. This is the person who keeps you focused and reminds you of the steps you have committed to taking towards your goal. It is the person who gives you the metaphorical kick in the butt to get going, helps you problem solve when obstacles are on your path, and is there to celebrate with you every step of the way.

One of the most important qualities an accountability buddy must possess is believing in you. They believe in you enough that they won't let you quit. They must care about you enough that they are willing to risk your disapproval to tell you what you need to hear. You want someone who will act like a coach, not a cop. A coach challenges you in a supportive manner, giving you inspiration and motivation, while a cop interrogates you and waits for you to screw up in order to serve you a ticket of shame and guilt.

To find a solid accountability buddy, you may want to hire a professional coach or mentor to provide you with an appropriate level of support. If this is not a viable option, create a list of everyone you know who possesses the following characteristics: reliable, trustworthy, responsible, motivated, committed, confidential, compassionate, perseveres, emotionally resilient (doesn't take things or what you say personally), accessible (can reach them 24/7), and someone who can relate to what you are going through, or what you are working towards.

Generally, I advise against using a family member or close friend as your main accountability buddy. There are a few reasons for this. Family and friends are more likely to let you slide, cheat, fall off the wagon, and not take you seriously. They see you how you have always been and resist you changing. Often, the changes you make affect them as well. Sometimes as we achieve success, they may become jealous or envious, thus creating even more obstacles for us. A man wanting to stop smoking may be offered a cigarette by his friend who continues to smoke, so that the friend is not feeling alone outside, or a failure himself. The wife who is trying to lose weight may prepare salads and healthier meal options, while the husband wants to go out for pizza or brings it home as a treat. Friends and family often don't have the same goals or motivation. Even if the changes you are making don't directly affect your friends or family, they may still unconsciously want to sabotage your efforts. They take any sign of weakness or soft spot as an indication that you don't really want the goal. Some examples of this are: "It's ok to splurge just this once; you have been working so hard, take a break; we are celebrating, you can start your diet again tomorrow; you look great, you don't need to watch what you eat; just one drink or smoke won't hurt," etc.

An accountability buddy would never say or do these things, but often our family and friends do. They are not trying to be mean; they just want us to be like we have always been, in the uncomfortable comfort zone. It is great to have family and friends on your team, no doubt about it. They should, however, be a secondary accountability buddy due to the lower success rates. This leads us to the question of: "Do I need to find just one perfect person for the job?" Of course not! I strongly advise you have at least two accountability buddies. Depending on what it is you are working towards, and how much external support you will require, you may find that you require four or five people to check in with. Some people find it helpful to have an accountability buddy in each area of their life, such as in the work place, at home, with a friend, etc.

Once you have an accountability buddy, or buddies, the next step is setting up a clear outline of each person's commitment, what support looks like for you, what steps the accountability buddy takes if you are not following through, how you will be in contact, and when you will communicate. Creating a contract of each person's roles and responsibilities minimizes struggles and miscommunication along the way.

Accountability is the glue that ties commitment to the result.
– Bob Proctor

Here is an example of how Tom used accountability buddies to assist him in releasing 50 pounds of excess weight. When Tom started out, he knew he needed several accountability buddies to keep him focused and on track. He wanted to go to the gym every morning and had struggled with this in the past. Tom created an agreement with his wife, Brenda, and his friend, Mark, to help him with this commitment. If Tom was still in bed by 6:30 a.m., his wife agreed to ask him if he was still planning on going to the gym. If he said no, she would gently remind him of his goals by using a key phrase that they had set up in advance. After that, it was up to Tom to make the choice whether to go or not. Brenda's job is not to do the work for Tom, only to support and encourage him. Tom's friend, Mark, supported him by meeting him at the gym. He would text Tom to remind him of his commitment if he had not heard from him by 6:45 a.m. to say that he was on his way.

Tom used another accountability buddy, Margaret, to support him in making healthy food choices. Weekly, Tom sent Margaret a record of what he ate and how he was feeling before, during, and after he consumed food. If she did not receive an email of the information by Friday night at 5 p.m., she would phone Tom to remind him of his commitment. Tom also checked in with Margaret mid-week to report his progress, celebrate his successes, and discuss struggles that arose. If he was struggling anytime during the week, he had the agreement with Margaret to phone or text her if he was about to make a poor choice. This is often referred to as a pattern interrupt. An accountability buddy is available at anytime the goal setter feels moments of temptation, in order to provide support during critical times. Tom frequently sat in front of the television in the evening eating junk food. Committing to contacting Margaret before he consumed a bag of potato chips assisted him in stopping the behaviour, and feeling supported during the process. Margaret's role during this time was to listen to how Tom was feeling, ask him if the choice he was about to make will get him closer to his goal, and brainstorm alternative, healthier ways of getting his needs met. Ultimately, Tom was still responsible for putting in the effort and making the choice of doing the work.

His accountability buddies merely remind him of his goals and action steps, work together to problem solve and celebrate his accomplishments with him. Use your accountability buddy for anything that will support you in stopping negative behaviours, starting positive behaviours, and celebrating successes.

Communication is key. Be clear on how you want them to challenge you and help push, pull, and sometimes drag you to the finish line. Without clear outlines beforehand, resentment, hurt feelings, frustration, and failure, will ultimately prevail.

Accountability breeds Response-Ability.
— Steven Covey

Homeplay: Accountability Contract

Time: 10-20 minutes

Purpose: To create a contract of clear guidelines, roles and responsibilities for both the goal setter and accountability buddy, with the intent of supporting one person in achieving a specific goal.

Materials Required: Paper, Pen, Contract, and Accountability Buddy

Exercise:

Complete the following contract or create one of your own with your chosen accountability buddy. Feel free to revise this contract and personalize it to suit your needs. It could also include: what happens when goal setter is not following through with their commitments; what happens when accountability buddy is not following through with their commitments; and/or a list of conditions in which to terminate the agreement. A downloadable form is available through stopquittingon yourself.com.

Relationship: Together is Better

Outcome Commitment Contract

Goal Setter Contact Information

Name: _____

Phone: _____

Email: _____

Accountability Buddy Contact Information

Name: _____

Phone: _____

Email: _____

I _____ (goal setter's name) have a specific goal that I am committed to working towards and require the support of an accountability buddy and a clear accountability system.

Thank you for being my accountability buddy! I am needing support to assist me in staying focused and on my path towards reaching my goals. Support looks like listening, pointing out what I can not or am not willing to see, and giving constructive feedback when I get sidetracked by indecision, fear or past behaviours. I will contact you in moments of doubt or temptation and be open to all feedback.

The role of the goal setter is to,

* Be honest with self-assessment.
* Be open and willing to ask for help and feedback.
* Check in with accountability buddy with results, successes and setbacks.
* Set goals, take action steps and implement a plan.
* Focus on results and action steps instead of excuses.
* Take action (even in spite of fear).
* Honouring the agreements in this contract.

The role of a support person is to,

* Actively listen
* Provide constructive feedback without judgement.
* Encourage reflection, action, and celebration.
* Hold goal setter accountable by following-up, being available and having the goal setters best interests at heart.
* Honouring the agreements in this contract.

Accountability schedule of goal setter:

* I will send you via _____ my desired outcomes, detailed action steps and plans, as well as rewards on or before _____.
* I will contact you via _____ on _____ to update my progress.
* I will contact you via _____ on _____ of each week/month to review and update my goals, action steps and plans.

Follow-up schedule of accountability buddy:

* If I have not heard from you by each specified date I will contact you to follow-up.

The role of accountability buddy is a volunteer process and can be terminated by the accountability buddy at any time. If the goal setter wishes to terminate this process, however he/she must provide a satisfactory reason to the accountability buddy and ask permission to end the contract.

I commit to this process!

_____
(Goal Setter Signature)

Date: _____

I commit to this process!

_____
(Accountability Buddy Signature)

Date: _____

Takeaway:

Choosing someone who is reliable to support others and does not back out of contracts and commitments is key. Hence, they need to be personally accountable themselves. The goal setter does not want to get into a situation where they need to be an accountability buddy for their accountability buddy. Having more than one accountability buddy proves essential, especially when working on goals with many aspects.

An accountability buddy is not responsible for another person's goal achievement or success. They are not there to rescue you, be your friend, or coddle you. View your relationship as a business or formal interaction. You wouldn't pat someone who works for you on the head and say, "There, there, poor baby, don't worry." No! The relationship is about staying focused on the facts at hand and working through the obstacles. Achieving your goals is up to you; choosing who you will have by your side along the way determines how quick, how easy, and how much fun the journey will be.

Personal Accountability

In order to be successful, a person needs to be personally accountable. Personally accountable means that there is no blame involved, and the person acknowledges his/her participation in getting the results in their lives, which gives them the power to look for the lessons and gifts in every situation. No blame means not blaming anyone or anything for your results or struggles, which includes yourself. In every situation, every struggle, every obstacle, and every interaction, there are lessons, gifts, and feedback to be learned. Without learning these, similar types of events will reoccur in our lives in order to provide other opportunities to get the awareness.

If no one is at fault, and we look at the event as neutral, meaning it is what it is, we can determine the lesson or gift from having this show up in our lives. Without being emotionally involved or charged about the situation, it is easier to see the flecks of gold in the dirt. Before Tom started on his weight release journey, he was given the news from his doctor informing him of being in the early stages of type 2 diabetes. The many extra pounds of weight, added over years, was the first opportunity for Tom to look for lessons and receive feedback. When he did nothing to change, life provided him a second opportunity with his diagnosis. Tom could have gone into victim mode, blaming his wife for not preparing healthy meals, which caused him to gain so much weight after they got married. Blaming others is not being personally accountable though. By pointing his finger at her, he knew there were three pointing back at him. He could have blamed himself for choosing to eat what she prepared, knowing that the types of meals she was cooking were high in calories. Placing blame on yourself is not being personally accountable either. He could have blamed his job for making him work long hours, not allowing enough time to exercise. Blaming keeps us in victim mode. When in victim mentality, we are not able to see how we participated to get the result, nor can we see the gifts that are now available because of the event or situation. Often, this is when excuses are the highest. Tom could have continued to use the excuse that he didn't have time to exercise or didn't know how to cook healthy meals. Tom knew, however, that excuses do not lead to success. He could have reasons, or results.

Tom surrendered to the situation to become personally accountable. He realized, no matter who he blamed for the state his body was in, it did not change anything. Blaming did not solve the problem. Blaming himself and others did not make him healthier. Focusing on what he should, or could, have done in the past is in the past. Past thinking is victim thinking. Focusing on the now is powerful as only the present situation is considered. He surrendered to the fact that his body was in poor health regardless of how it happened. Surrender to what is, and let go of imaginary, alternative circumstances. Often, when we are fresh in an event, we cannot see the lessons or gifts. Sometimes the gifts evolve over time.

Due to this diagnosis, Tom formed some of the most powerful, nurturing, and life-long relationships with his accountability buddies and mentors. He learned how to ask for support and be open to receiving feedback. This improved his relationships with his family and led to promotions at work. Through his commitment to himself, he is healthier now than he was before he got married, and he has more self-confidence and self-esteem than ever before. Tom's weight release journey also opened doors for him that he never thought possible, such as being asked to coach others on how to successfully release weight, publishing a recipe book, and running a half marathon with his son. None of these events would have transpired if Tom had chosen to stay in victim mentality and refused to become personally accountable.

You are not stuck where you are unless you decide to be.
– Wayne Dyer

Homeplay: Excuses Be Gone

Time: 5-10 minutes

Purpose: To get clear on the thoughts and excuses that stop you from achieving your goal.

Materials Required: Paper and Pen

Exercise:

1. Make a list of excuses that you have been using that are stopping you from getting to your goal. The best way to do this is to ask yourself, "I want _____, but..." How do you finish this sentence? This is the part where you say you want something, then the "yeah, but..." starts appearing. These are the stories and excuses that you have made up in your head of why you can't achieve your goals and what is standing in the way. They are nothing more than made up stories you created to keep yourself in the uncomfortable comfort zone.

2. For each excuse, brainstorm reasons why that is not true, and how you can overcome the excuse. How can you move past this obstacle on your path?

Example: I want to earn more money, but...

Excuse: I don't know how.

Solution: Find a mentor, read books, take night classes to climb the ladder at work, talk to an investor, research, talk to successful people.

<u>Excuse</u>: I don't have time.

<u>Solution</u>: Stop watching reality television, listen to audiobooks on my commute to work, ask for help from others, hire a financial coach, delegate other jobs and responsibilities, limit my time on social media and the internet, implement a time management system.

<u>Excuse</u>: I don't have any money to invest.

Solution: Research no money down investment options, look at getting a loan, find a mentor willing to coach either free or at a reduced rate, create and stick to a budget, monitor my spending, stop buying unnecessary things, start a savings account.

Takeaway:

Commit to eliminating excuses from your thoughts by focusing on how to solve the problem rather than focusing on the problem itself. The captain of a ship doesn't see an obstacle in the way and just throw their hands in the air to give up. He/she does what it takes to move through the storm. Only you can choose whether you will dance in the rain or grumble about it. You can have excuses, or you can have results. What are you choosing?

Chapter 3: Key Concepts

- If you don't love yourself, no one else can truly love you.
- Loving yourself starts with accepting who you are.
- When you try to be everything to everybody, you end up being nothing to nobody.
- There is no better reason and no excuse big enough that trumps self-love.
- People do not like you for what you do for them; they love you for how you make them feel.
- We become our environment. Surround yourself with positive, uplifting people to increase your energy and positive thoughts.
- The power of positive people pays off.
- The goal may seem out of reach or difficult to reach from where you are standing, but having a team of support helping lift you up and over the obstacles standing in your way is immeasurable.
- Accountability buddies remind you of your goals and action steps, work together to problem solve, and celebrate your accomplishments with you.
- Achieving your goals is up to you; choosing who you will have by your side along the way determines how quick, how easy, and how much fun the journey will be.
- Excuses do not lead to success. You can have the reasons, or the results.
- In every situation, every struggle, every obstacle, and every interaction, there are lessons, gifts and feedback, if you are open to receiving.
- Only you can choose whether you will dance in the storm or let the storm inside. Either way, be personally accountable.

Chapter 4

Re-Write: Old Thought Patterns

Wouldn't it be great if you could just go into your mind and erase the negative messages that keep playing? Wouldn't life be easier if you could replace negative self-talk with positive messages? What if I said it is possible, that there is a method that can do all of this and more? It can make replacing poor habits with good habits feel automatic, so you don't have to consciously think about it. It can make taking the necessary action steps feel natural and easy. Sound too good to be true? Oh, did I mention this all happens while you are sitting or lying down comfortably, possibly even sleeping! It is one of the most powerful ways to create change in your life as it works with changing your mindset first. Remember: thoughts -> feelings -> behaviours/habits = your results.

The Science of Mind

Hypnosis has long been associated with participants performing on stage and being 'under the control' of a hypnotist. Brainwashing, loss of control, and fear of the unknown are in the forefront of sceptic minds. While hypnosis can be used as a form of entertainment, it is also an extremely powerful tool for creating new possibilities in alternative medicine and behaviour modification. Incredible feats have been done using the power of the mind under hypnosis. For years, people did not know how or why it worked, leaving assumptions and false beliefs to be fabricated. With modern science, however, we now have the knowledge and understanding to support the extraordinary acts that have been accomplished. The use of hypnosis is not a recent discovery, or practice, and is rapidly expanding in credibility and popularity. Hypnotic trances have been used for hundreds of years and were documented in almost every ancient civilization. In the mid-1800's, Dr. James Esdaile performed over 300 painless surgeries using only hypnosis for medication. You may be wondering why I am telling you this and how it is applicable to you in your situation right now. If the mind is so powerful it can free the body from pain while being cut open, do you think it is powerful enough to help you stop eating junk food, quit smoking, or get you to whatever it is you are wanting? Absolutely!

Now, your mind may be doing the "yeah, but..."—it wouldn't work for me; I can't be hypnotized; I don't want walk around like a zombie; if hypnosis is so great, why isn't it used more?—or some version of this, am I right?

Dispelling Myths

Understanding how and why hypnosis works is the first step in dismissing some of the preconceived beliefs and associations the public has with hypnosis. There are many common misconceptions that have been formed around hypnosis. The reason for these myths vary in origin but include stories being passed on from generation to generation, watching entertainment in the form of stage hypnosis, or the misrepresentation in movies. The main resistance people have towards hypnosis is the fear of the unknown, not knowing if they will come out of hypnosis, being made to share their deepest darkest secrets, not being able to remember anything, and, the most common one, not wanting to be under the control of someone else! All of these myths are easily diminished with the proper education. Understanding how or why something works is important to minimizing our fear. Humans are programmed to fear that which is unknown to them. People who experience hypnosis enjoy the practice and are curious to learn more, particularly patients that have used hypnosis for surgical procedures.

One of the most reoccurring fears is individuals are completely under the control of the hypnotist. This could not be further from the truth! In fact, all hypnosis is self-hypnosis. A hypnotist cannot hypnotize a person without their participation. Patients, or participants in the case of stage performances, are choosing to be hypnotized. No one can be hypnotized unless they choose to be, nor will they do anything that is against their deepest moral beliefs. This may be the reason why, during some stage hypnosis shows, participants come out of their hypnotic state and are asked to leave the stage. Hypnotized individuals will not share anything that they do not want to share, or do anything that they are morally against. As an example, a participant would not rob a bank if a hypnotist suggested for them to do so, unless of course they already had plans to!

Brainwashing is often associated with hypnosis, but it is different. Brainwashing involves being denied basic needs, such as food, water, and sleep, while being indoctrinated with commands involuntarily. In hypnotherapy, individuals are aware of what will be suggested to them and they willingly choose to participate.

Other common myths are that an individual will never wake up or come out of hypnosis, or that it is scary. Hypnosis is a very relaxed state, and everyone goes in and out of hypnosis throughout their day. In fact, a light form of hypnosis is daydreaming. Driving on a regular route and arriving, not recalling the trip, was a hypnotic experience! The subconscious mind was in the driver's seat, while the conscious mind was off thinking about other things. This is hypnosis. Hypnosis is simply a narrow focus of mind. Anytime one is engrossed in an activity when they lose concept of time, or even their surroundings, they are in a state of hypnosis. Crying, reading a book, watching television, or doing a hobby are all common examples of when people are in hypnotic states.

Another misconception is that hypnosis is a magic pill. Hypnosis can have very high success rates in goal achievement. Without having the desire to make changes, and the belief that what you are doing will work, no modality will be of benefit to a person, including hypnosis. Everybody can be hypnotized, if they want to be.

Hypnosis and meditation are actually the same state, which is often misunderstood. The only difference is the intention behind each act. Meditation is used to quiet the mind, and hypnosis is used to focus the mind to achieve a desired result. Meditation is a passive state, whereas hypnosis is a more active state of mind. Fifteen minutes of either of these activities is equal to four hours of sleep. It is not a replacement for sleep, however, as the body still requires deep sleep, or delta sleep.

The single most powerful asset we have is our mind.
If trained well, it can create enormous wealth.
– Robert Kiyosaki

The Science Behind

We experience resistance to something when we feel fearful or uncertain. To understand and relieve some of that, here is a brief scientific explanation of how your brain physically changes when you want to create new thought patterns or behaviours. The brain is made of tiny nerve cells called neurons. These neurons have tiny branches that reach out and connect to other neurons to form what is known as a neuro net. Each place where they connect is integrated into a thought or memory. The more a repeated thought or memory is processed, the more branches, and the bigger and stronger the connection.

This means if you have a repeated negative thought of "I'm stupid," that connection in the neuro net gets stronger and becomes more of a reality. That belief of "I'm stupid" might lead to struggling with remembering information, having a low self-esteem, or creating fear of wanting to try new things. On the other hand, if you have a repeated, positive thought such as, "I am smart and capable," your life experiences will be much different because of the belief and strength of that connection. Does that make sense?

Given that the connections are thoughts or memories, it does not matter if it actually happened or if we just created it in our minds. The brain does not know whether an event actually happened or if we just imagined it happening, because the same neurons are firing. Since it doesn't know the difference between imagination and reality, we can use our imagination to create new neural connections! Scientists call this neuroplasticity, meaning the brain can physically change due to real or imagined experiences. Repeated positive suggestions, such as those used in hypnotherapy, cause neurons to fire and link together, creating change to the connections in your brain and the behaviours in your life! The more neurons that form into a neuro net, the stronger and more automatic the belief or habit. The stronger the neuro net, the easier it will be to create changes in your behaviours. If cells no longer have repeated energy linking them together, they lose their long-term relationship and connection. How you think is the difference between success and failure, between taking action and not, between getting what you want and staying stuck. Henry Ford said it best, "Whether you think you can or think you can't, you are right."

What we think creates our reality. Through the use of hypnosis, reforming our neuro net structures can heal our minds and bodies, and create the required beliefs and behaviours needed to live our dreams and desires.

What you think, you become. What you feel, you attract.
What you imagine, you create.
– Buddha

How Hypnosis Works

Knowing that repeated positive thoughts can change the neuro nets in your mind, you may wonder why hypnosis is required. Why can't you just say positive messages to yourself and change the connections in your mind? Affirmations are positive statements repeated frequently with the intent of changing beliefs and thought patterns. While using affirmations can be powerful, they are often not very effective. The following explains the components of our mind and why trying to change our thoughts and behaviours at a conscious level creates frustration and failure.

Our mind is made up of a conscious mind (1–10%) and a subconscious mind (90–99%). It is very much like an iceberg. The conscious mind is the part we are aware of and can see on top of the water. The subconscious mind is the larger part, under the water, that we are unaware of.

Our conscious mind is responsible for analyzing and making decisions; hence the saying, making a 'conscious choice.' While functioning from the conscious mind, we are aware of what we are thinking. When saying positive affirmations, we are using our conscious mind. Unfortunately, the conscious mind only holds information for an hour or two, making it very difficult to change habits or behaviours using this part of the mind only.

The subconscious mind is the largest part of our mind, is the most critical, and is often underestimated. It is the part under the surface that we are not consciously aware of. Its job is to accept all information whether it is true, false, or imagined. It does not analyze or interpret whether information is useful or helpful, it simply stores the messages. The subconscious mind is like a large filing cabinet with different folders for each area and experience in your life.

You operate subconsciously when you do things automatically, like getting dressed in the morning. You don't have to think, "Alright now, which foot should I put into the pant leg first?" You just do it. You have repeated your morning getting ready for the day routine so many times that it becomes automatic. You don't have to consciously think about it anymore, so your subconscious mind takes over as the process is stored there. When toddlers are getting dressed, it is a new experience and habit for them, so they need to consciously make decisions, like which foot to put the sock on. This obviously takes them longer to complete the task. However, as adults, when you are running on automatic pilot, a.k.a. your subconscious mind, this allows your conscious mind to think about other things, such as important tasks for the day ahead. When you repeatedly do the same action, you begin to use your subconscious mind instead of your conscious mind. This is the reason many people have trouble consciously remembering if they turned the coffee pot off in the mornings, or locked the door, because they were running on autopilot and not really consciously aware of what they were doing.

What happens when we have behaviours stored in our subconscious mind that are unsupportive? Is sitting on the couch eating junk food in the evening, a habit that has become automatic? Is reaching for a cigarette, when you get into the vehicle, a subconscious automatic habit? What unsupportive habits do you have automatically happen without you consciously making the choice?

Homeplay: Unsupportive Habits

Time: 10-15 minutes

Purpose: To become aware of negative, unsupportive habits that occur automatically, which you are not consciously choosing.

Materials Required: Paper and Pen

Exercise:

Feel free to close your eyes while you visualize the following scenario. Imagine you are lying in bed sleeping and you are about to wake up for the day. On this day, however, you know that all your unsupportive habits will be exaggerated, so you can easily recognize them. What is the first thing you do when you open your eyes? What are you thinking? Do you have thoughts like, "Ugh, I hate mornings; I hate my life; I wish it was the weekend; etc." Do you hit the snooze button on your alarm clock repeatedly? What thoughts are you thinking that make you do this? As the exaggerated, unsupportive habits show up in your day, write them down on your piece of paper. Continue imagining going through your day, becoming aware of all negative habits and self-talk that occurs.

Takeaway:

You may choose to do this visualization a few times. Designating one day to focus on negative thoughts and habits that pop up can also be effective at becoming more aware. Remember, awareness is power. What you do with that awareness is up to you! Using hypnosis and other techniques found in this book will be a helpful way at rewriting those thoughts and changing those unsupportive behaviours.

As information comes in through the conscious mind and drops into the subconscious mind, it is filtered through an important component called the critical area. The critical area is both conscious and subconscious, and serves as a large filter. It filters information according to what we believe to be true. Consciously saying a positive affirmation to yourself, when you actually believe the opposite to be true, will not provide you with any results, as the information you are feeding your mind is being discarded. Beliefs are the gatekeepers of information getting into your subconscious mind and the pivotal force behind your choices and behaviours.

The thoughts we think and the words
we speak create our experiences.
– Louise Hay

Living Life With the Mind of a Child

Beliefs are stored in both the conscious and subconscious mind and are simply statements that are true to you. This means we are consciously aware of some of the beliefs we have and we are not aware of others. If you think back to when we compared the mind to an iceberg, some beliefs are above the water, allowing us to see and be aware of them, and some beliefs are hiding below the water, without us knowing they are there.

Belief systems are in place to protect us from potential dangers and anything unfamiliar to us. They are either empowering or disempowering. They are formed between the ages of 5 and 12 years of age, and we live our lives based on what we believe. So, basically, we are functioning and filtering our lives, as adults, based on a belief system we created in our minds as a child. It might need some updating, yes?

Since every choice, decision, action, and thought you have is filtered by your belief system, it is crucial that your beliefs are supportive and positive, wouldn't you say? If you want to create supportive automatic behaviours, you need the messages that get filtered down into your subconscious mind to be positive, so that the automatic pilot is functioning from a positive space.

For example, if you have the belief of I am ugly, when someone tells you, "You are beautiful," it will be rejected by your belief system, and that positive message will not go into your subconscious mind. That statement, "You are beautiful," will be rejected or discarded because it does not align with what you believe to be true. The result of this is you feeling uncomfortable and dismissing the statement by disagreeing or blowing it off. Since the message is not in alignment with what you believe to be true, you keep operating from the belief I am ugly, or stupid, or whatever—you fill in the blank. With hypnosis, however, we are able to bypass the filters to plant the positive, empowering suggestions directly into the subconscious mind and rewrite beliefs in the critical area. This makes the mind think differently, so, when someone tells you, "You are beautiful," this will align with your belief system, making it feel true, and you feel beautiful.

Saying positive affirmations to yourself when they are not in alignment with your belief system is like trying to chip your way through a door with a butter knife. Hypnosis is like having the key to open the door. Quicker and more effective, yes?

This is a simple example, but imagine how productive, healthy and enjoyable your life would be if the sabotaging negative beliefs were replaced with powerful ones! Unconscious fear and beliefs stand in the way of your success.

There is a story of a baby elephant who, when it was very young, was trained not to wander away. The trainer tied a rope around the baby elephant's leg, which led to a stake in the ground. The elephant learned from a young age that it was not strong enough to break the rope. It was conditioned to stay close to the stake in the ground. Of course, as the elephant grew, it became strong enough to break the rope. Since it had learned from a young age that it was not strong enough, the adult elephant did not even try. Humans do the same thing in their lives by limiting how far they can go, based on years of believing a story that is no longer true. How many times do you let limiting beliefs hold you back from what you want? Are you playing small in your life because of a belief you created as a child?

Many people, including myself years ago, say "I'll believe it when I see it." In reality, the exact opposite is true—you'll see it when you believe it. When you believe you can achieve your goals, you will. That is how powerful beliefs and your mind are. It is that simple. So, what are you choosing to believe?

Believe you can and you are half way there.
– Theodore Roosevelt

Homeplay: Unsupportive Beliefs

Time: 10-15 minutes

Purpose: To identify what beliefs are keeping you from achieving your goals.

Materials Required: Paper and Pen

Exercise:

Using the awarenesses from previous Homeplay exercises, or simply brainstorming, make a list of all the negative, unsupportive beliefs that are holding you back from achieving your goals. Here is a list of common beliefs that clients have discovered while doing this exercise:

- I am not good enough
- I am not smart enough
- Fear of rejection
- Fear of success
- Fear of failure
- I am unlovable
- I am powerless
- I am not safe
- I am all alone
- I am unwanted
- I am unworthy
- I am unimportant
- I am inferior
- I can't change
- I am always wrong

- Life isn't fair
- I can't trust people
- I will never be rich
- I will never be successful
- I don't deserve anything
- Nothing good ever happens to me

Create a list of 5–10 beliefs that resonate with you the most. Then change the statement into a positive, empowering one. This can usually be done by simply taking out the negative words such as not, never, can't, don't, etc.

Write the 5–10 empowering statements on a piece of paper. Put them up around your house, in your car, and anywhere that you will see them. I encourage you to consciously read them at least five times every day, as well as subconsciously read them throughout the day. By subconsciously reading them, I am referring to your subconscious mind seeing them without you consciously stopping to read them. Your subconscious mind is taking in information while your conscious mind is off thinking about other things, so use that to your advantage. The more your mind is aware of the positive messages, the better. Once you have the belief that the affirmation is true, repeating the affirmation will strengthen the neuro nets in your mind, making the belief more powerful to create what it is you want in your life.

Takeaway:

Beliefs are not true or false. They are simply made up statements we use to filter experiences through. We are story telling machines! Nothing means anything, except the meaning we give it. Every event is neutral; it is only our perception and beliefs that filter what we see and interpret. Beliefs affect the choices we make in our lives, and, ultimately, the results we achieve. When you accept and believe that you are worthy and deserving of your goals, nothing can stop you from success. What are you choosing to believe?

You see things; and you say, "Why?" But I dream things that never were; and I say, "Why not?"
– George Bernard Shaw

The Most Productive Sleep

Hypnosis is a scientific state that can be measured by an EEG machine. However, without a machine to prove that a person is in a hypnotic state, there are some physical symptoms that often occur indicating a certain level of hypnotic trance. Everyone will experience a state of hypnosis in their own specific way because everyone is unique.

Just like the two minutes before falling asleep at night, while one is in a hypnotic state, being formally hypnotized has similar physical sensations. Hypnotized individuals can hear everything the hypnotherapist is saying, be in complete control, remember everything (unless it is suggested otherwise), and will be able to speak and move around. A hypnotic state can produce a feeling of heaviness or lightness in one's body or extremities, tingling in hands or feet, general body relaxation, sensitive hearing, slowing down of breathing rate and pulse rate, change in body temperature, and swallowing. It is common for people to feel dissociated from parts of their body. Time can seem distorted when in hypnosis; some feel it goes by very quickly while others feel as though time slows down. Time distortion is common when hypnotically driving, such as feeling as though the trip went by quickly. All these are common signs that a person is experiencing a hypnotic state.

Since hypnosis is not dangerous and has no negative side effects, it is useful for everyone, regardless of their age. Hypnosis is also useful for just about any symptom. It can be used as an alternative medicine or a preventative one.

I have included a few hypnosis scripts for you. Use these scripts to hypnotize yourself! As an alternative, I have many specific hypnosis audios available on my website www.lightenuptherapy.ca. The best part of a hypnosis audio is you can listen to it as you go to bed at night. Your subconscious mind is always listening, even when your conscious mind is off with Mr. Sandman. Change your thoughts and beliefs into positive, empowering ones, while you sleep. It is the most productive sleep you will have!

Homeplay: Hypnosis Scripts

All hypnosis is self-hypnosis, meaning you are in complete control! Find a comfortable and quiet place where you won't be disturbed. I suggest you shut off your phone, ask anyone who lives with you to not enter the room, and create a place of peace for the next 20–60 minutes. If you feel tired and are worried you might fall asleep, set an alarm to make sure you are awake at your designated time. Hypnosis is not technically sleeping, although it is the Greek meaning. You can lie down or sit in a reclining chair, or anywhere that you can be comfortable and at ease. If you find yourself falling asleep before finishing the script, choose a less comfortable position such as sitting upright, or doing it earlier in the day when you are not as tired. On the other hand, if you are struggling to focus or relax your body, starting with a pre-recorded audio can be helpful. As you practice self-hypnosis, you may find that a few intentional deep breathes is all it takes to get you in a hypnotic trance. Enjoy the deep relaxation and peace of hypnosis!

Script 1: Special Spot

Step 1: Deep Breathing
I want you to think of the word relax, as you begin to focus on your breath. The word relax has two syllables, re and lax. As you breathe in through your nose, deeply and smoothly, think of the syllable, re. As you exhale through your mouth, think of the last syllable, laaax. On the exhale, release any tension or stress you may be holding in your body. Allow each breath to be smooth and deep, filling up your lungs completely on the inhale and expelling all the air on the exhale. Continue to do this sequence of breath several times, focusing on the word, relax. As you focus on the word, feel your body and mind become more relaxed and comfortable.

Step 2: Special Spot Visualization
In your mind, imagine, see, or pretend that you are in a place that is very safe and comforting—a place that is special and makes you feel relaxed and serene. This can be a place you have been before, or somewhere you just imagine. Feel the pleasure and tranquility as you surround yourself with the perfect setting. Look around and see what is there in your special place. What do you hear? Are there any smells? In your mind's eye, please reach out and touch something. It does not matter what it is—

a piece of furniture, a flower, water, a blanket. Touch it, just so you know it is there. Imagine drawing in all the empowering energy right into the core of your being. Feel yourself lighter, more relaxed, and more grounded through that connection. Feel how comforted you are just by being in this place. Fill yourself up with the comfort and serenity this place provides, so you feel safe and secure, and always in complete control.

Step 3: Count Down 5 to 1
In a moment, count DOWN from 5 down to 1. When you get to the last number, say the words DEEPLY RELAXED. When you hear the words DEEPLY RELAXED, feel your body become so completely relaxed that you will feel like every muscle is melting like butter.

5 – Feel your body becoming more relaxed and comforted with each word, feeling as though your entire body is sinking down into the chair or bed.

4 – Allow the feeling of safety and security to spread throughout your body and mind, as you relax even deeper now.

3 – Imagine any tension or worries drifting away like clouds in the sky. Drifting away, drifting away now. As they drift away, you find your body and mind become two, then three times more relaxed.

2 – Pretend for a moment that your entire body is like a feather, just floating and drifting down, drifting down into a soft comfortable pillow. Feel your mind and body at complete rest now.

1 – DEEPLY RELAXED!

Step 4: Positive Affirmations

Note: For this step, create your own personal list of positive statements that will assist you in taking action to achieve your goals. Homeplay exercises, you have completed earlier, are a great place to start.

Repeat positive affirmations at least five times for each statement.

Step 5: Count Up 1 to 5

In a moment, you are going to count from 1 up to 5. When you get to the number 5, you can open your eyes, have a good stretch, and say aloud the words, WONDERFULLY REFRESHED (or another short power phrase of your choosing).

1 – Slowly bringing your awareness back to the room and your surroundings.

2 – Taking a deep breath in through your nose, and exhale through your mouth. Feeling refreshed and invigorated in both mind and body.

3 – Feeling incredibly good from the top of your head all the way down to the tips of your toes.

4 – Begin to wiggle your fingers and toes, feeling confidence and motivation spread throughout your body.

5 – Take your time, when you are ready, open your eyes, stretch your body, and say aloud the words, WONDERFULLY REFRESHED (or whatever power phrase you chose).

Step 6: Affirmations
Declare out loud, 5–10 positive affirmations that will help you achieve your goals. Repeat each affirmation at least five times.

Script 2: Cloud of Comfort

Step 1: Deep Breathing
In a moment, you are going to take some deep breaths. As you take these breaths, imagine breathing in a white light that brings a feeling of tranquility and serenity. As you exhale, feel and imagine all the tension, discomfort, and stress leave your body. Some people see the exhale as a dark mist or black cloud. Whatever you imagine or see is perfect for you. There is no right or wrong way to do this, just feel your body relaxing and becoming more comfortable with each breath. Focus on breathing in a white healing light that spreads to every part of your body while exhaling any dark tension or stress. Do this several times before going to the next step.

Step 2: Progressive Muscle Relaxation
Focus on the muscles in your forehead, and feel them relax down the more you focus on them. Feel the muscles around your eyes softening. Feel the relaxation spread into your cheeks and jaw muscles. Feel your jaw muscles release and your jaw sink down. The more you try to resist them relaxing, the more relaxed they will become. Moving the relaxation down into your neck. Relaxing every muscle, every nerve, every fibre in your neck now. Down into your shoulders. Feeling like the weight of the world is coming off your shoulders, and just let it go. Let the weight of the world come off your shoulders as you feel your shoulders relax down. Like waves in the ocean, feel waves of relaxation going down both arms. All the way down to your

fingertips. The muscles in your chest have already begun to become more relaxed; see if you can relax them even more now. Down into stomach the relaxation spreads. Down into your thighs. Feeling every muscle in your thighs relax down and become comfortable. Spread the relaxation down into your knees, down into your shins and your calves, down into your ankles and all the way through to the tips of your toes. Feel waves of comfort from the top of your head all the way down to the tips of your toes. It feels so good to relax and let go.

Step 3: Staircase
Imagine yourself at the top of a beautiful wooden staircase, descending down to a white sandy beach. Notice there is a safe and sturdy handrail on both sides of the staircase. In a moment, begin walking down these stairs, and, as you do, feel your body and mind becoming more relaxed and comfortable with each step. When you get to the last step, say the words, DEEPLY RELAXED, to go into a deep state of hypnosis. When you are ready, take your first step down the stairs.

10 – Taking your first step down the stairs as you hold the handrails for safety and security.

9 – Feeling confident that you can accomplish anything you put your mind to.

8 – Seeing the bright blue water and white sandy beach at the bottom of the stairs.

7 – Feeling relaxed and happy as you make your way down the stairs one step at a time.

6 – Knowing that you are worthy and capable of your goals.

5 – Feeling more and more relaxed and confident with each step.

4 – Hearing the sounds of the waves lapping up on the shore and the birds flying overhead.

3 – Feeling the warmth of the sun and a gentle breeze warming you to the perfect temperature.

2 – Allowing your mind and body to relax into the comfort and serenity.

1 – DEEPLY RELAXED

Step 4: Positive Affirmations
Note: For this step, create your own personal list of positive statements that will assist you in taking action to achieve your goals. Homeplay exercises, you have completed already, are a great place to start.

Repeat positive affirmations at least five times for each statement.

Step 5: Count Up 1 to 5
In a moment, you are going to count from 1 up to 5. When you get to the number 5, you can open your eyes, have a good stretch, and say aloud the words, WONDERFULLY REFRESHED (or another short power phrase of your choosing).

1 – Slowly bringing your awareness back to the room and your surroundings.

2 – Taking a deep breath in through your nose, and exhale through your mouth. Feeling refreshed and invigorated in both mind and body.

3 – Feeling incredibly good from the top of your head all the way down to the tips of your toes.

4 – Begin to wiggle your fingers and toes, feeling confidence and motivation spread throughout your body.

5 – Take your time, when you are ready, open your eyes, stretch your body, and say aloud the words, WONDERFULLY REFRESHED (or whatever power phrase you chose).

Step 6: Affirmations
Declare out loud 5–10 positive affirmations that will help you achieve your goals. Repeat each affirmation at least five times.

Success Stories

My first personal success story using hypnosis was being able to fly in an airplane without getting motion sickness. Now, this may not seem like that big of deal for most people, but, for me, hypnosis changed my life. Every time I flew anywhere, I was sick, and anyone who had ever flown with me, knows that this is the understatement of the century. I was the girl who was geared up with the extremely fashionable wristbands to "prevent" motion sickness. Airport security guards would quizzically stare at my overflowing bag of medications that I inhaled like they were going to save my life. I looked like I was in a bad accident with all the anti-motion sickness patches I wore. Oblivious to the looks of horror from my neighbouring travellers, as soon as I was seated I frantically searched the seat pocket in front of me (and theirs as well), to ensure we all had clean white bags to throw up in. Walking to the bathroom was often not an option, as I was too sick and dizzy to even stand up. Despite all of my efforts to prevent the dreaded experience, I was frequently wheeled away from the plane in a wheelchair and given oxygen, after using up what I can only imagine to be an airline's years' worth of barf bags. I apologize to any airline stewardesses and fellow passengers reading this book that had to endure my situation at 30,000 feet. The entire first day of a vacation was ruined as my body took that long to recover from the experience. Not only was the first day ruined, but the last couple of days before I was to return home were stressful. The anticipation of the plane ride home felt terrible and frightening. It wasn't like I only sometimes got sick; it was inevitable. When it was time to go on my honeymoon, I had decided I was not going to let motion sickness wreck my trip. I had a 12 hour flight, followed by two small island hopper flights, to make it to Bora Bora. There was no way I was turning down paradise to drive somewhere snowy, cold, and close by in Canada! After only one hypnosis session with a certified hypnotherapist, the flights were fantastic! I never threw up, and I walked off the plane ready to celebrate! Today, I fly with no anxiety, stress, sickness, medication, wristbands, or patches. All I need with me is my personal hypnosis audio and a ticket to somewhere tropical!

The following are a few testimonials from clients I have worked with who used hypnosis to change some aspect of their lives.

When I heard about hypnosis and how it helped people quit smoking, I was, to be perfectly honest, very skeptical, and a little scared! I didn't want some stranger messing with my brain and thoughts, and I had the misconception that the hypnotist could program you to do whatever they wanted. After doing further research, and sitting in on my daughters first session; I mean, why not, if you are nervous about something, send the kids in first!!! My daughter's session went extremely well. Since, she experienced such a positive change, I decided to book myself in as well. It works!! I have been smoke free for just over ten months and loving every minute of it. My daughter, who struggled with test anxiety and a lack of self-confidence, is also enjoying an extremely positive improvement in her life. She is doing fabulous, and we could not be happier for her. Hypnosis has done some fabulous things for our family, and, if you have a struggle that you could use help with, I highly recommend you give hypnosis a try. – Laurie Heck

I would recommend hypnotherapy to anyone serious about becoming a non-smoker, because it worked for me with no uncomfortable withdrawals. – Gloria Morrison

Hypnotherapy is a way to change habits, beliefs, and attitudes, at a core level. It can help you understand WHY you do things and shift that to get better results in your life. It is a harmless and easy way to get more long lasting results in your life for the change that you seek. – Crystal Wimpney

I didn't know if it would work for me. I tried stage hypnosis and it never worked, so I figured it just wasn't for me. During hypnosis, I felt very relaxed and in complete control the whole time. After hypnosis, I was on such a high, thinking, "Who wouldn't want to do this?!" It taught me how to relax and stay in control throughout pregnancy and childbirth. – Kimberly Walsh

After hypnosis, I felt like I had shed most of my past so I could move forward to a new me, without any of the baggage that had accumulated from my marriage and relationships before marriage. – Corey Lee

Chapter 4: Key Concepts

- Humans are programmed to fear that which is unknown to them.
- The brain doesn't know the difference between imagination and reality, so we can use our imagination to create new neural connections!
- What we think, creates our reality.
- The conscious mind only holds information for an hour or two, making it very difficult to change habits or behaviours, using this part of the mind only.
- We live our lives based on what we believe.
- Unconscious fear and beliefs stand in the way of your success.
- Beliefs are not true or false. They are simply made up statements we use to filter experiences through.
- Nothing means anything, except the meaning we give it. Every event is neutral; it is only our perception and beliefs that filter what we see and interpret.
- Beliefs affect the choices we make in our lives, and, ultimately, the results we achieve.
- All hypnosis is self-hypnosis, meaning you are in complete control!

Chapter 5

Repeat: Rituals and Habits

Let's do a quick recap. By this point in the book, you should have clearly outlined what it is you want, and why, with specific daily, weekly, and monthly action steps. You have created an agreement with a qualified accountability buddy to assist you, and gathered a group of like-minded people to surround yourself with. You now also have tools for changing your negative thoughts and beliefs into positive empowering ones.

This chapter is all about creating and implementing daily rituals and habits that keep you in the energy of success and motivation. When you have positive energy and feel good, you will be more creative, more productive, more motivated and more successful. Have you ever noticed this? When you feel happy, you have more energy, and when you have more energy, you tend to get more accomplished. Feelings of overwhelm, discouragement, and depression, on the other hand, often leads to unsupportive habits such as sitting on the couch watching mindless reality TV and eating potato chips. Hence, no forward momentum towards your goal.

In Chapter 1, you learned that thoughts->feelings->behaviours=results. Changing the way you think will not happen overnight. It is a process, although it can happen quickly using hypnosis. Sometimes, waiting and being patient for the changes to become automatic is not helpful when 'shit hits the fan.' In times like this, we need something quick and immediate. Learning and implementing daily rituals and habits, that allow you to shift your energy into a space of inspiration, relaxation or vibrant energy, is key to being consistent and focused.

Have you ever had the experience of having a great day until you got a phone call that put you in a bad mood instantly? Maybe it was opening a piece of mail or an email. Whatever the reason, having your energy shift to negative, quickly, can disrupt the momentum and trajectory for your day, yes? Well, that is true only if you choose it to be.

Instead of being thrown off course and distracted, the following tools and techniques will provide you with practical steps to get your energy and mood to exactly where you want and need it to be, and keep it there.

What we think, we become.
– Buddha

Review and Reflect

Without reviewing and reflecting on your progress, how will you know where you are in relation to your goal? How will you know if you need to adjust certain steps along the way? How will you know when to celebrate your successes?

When moving towards a goal, it is common to keep your nose on the grindstone, working diligently and relentlessly. I call this the Mole Syndrome. If moles are tunnelling under the ground and want to get to a specific destination, they need to stop, look up, and recalibrate where they are in relation to their goal. Otherwise, they will end up going in circles, backtracking, and wasting time. They will expel energy needlessly, ultimately never reaching their goal. Do you work like a mole? Do you feel like you are running around, putting out fires and just trying to check the next thing off the to-do list? Do you feel like you are working hard and not making progress? Moles are near-sighted, meaning they only see what is right in front of them. This is like trying to make it home in the dark with only a flashlight. It is easy to go off track and lose direction when all you can ever see is the next step in front of you.

There are also goal setters that I refer to as Floaters. These types of people are solely focused on the end goal and don't want to be brought down by everyday tasks and commitments. They are often several steps ahead in their mind compared to where they are in reality. This causes them to continually waste time, energy, and money. Floaters are often redoing tasks because they were not done properly the first time, or steps were skipped. It may feel as though they are being chained down, while desperately struggling to break free. Floaters are far-sighted, meaning they only focus on what is in the distance. This is like trying to make it home in the dark with only a lighthouse shining your way. It is easy to get discouraged and give up when all you can see is your destination, but none of the steps to get there.

Moles and Floaters experience many struggles and frustrations. To break free of being near or far sighted, in relation to your goals, it is essential to review and reflect. Review where you are currently, where you want to end up, and uncover the quickest and easiest path to your destination. This is the job of a navigator. The most straight forward path from point A to point B may not be the best choice. While staying committed to your goals is essential, staying on a path, just because it was the one you chose at the beginning, is not always a smart choice. Weaving around obstacles and barriers can be less stressful, time consuming, and financially draining, than trying to push through or climb over them.

Looking up to see upcoming challenges on your path will save you time, money, and headaches. Making consistent adjustments along the way creates an effortless and enjoyable journey to your destination. Create the habit of reviewing what it is you say you want on a daily basis. This keeps your intention fresh in your conscious mind, making it easier for you to take action steps towards the goal. Reviewing your goals, and the reasons you want those goals, on a daily basis, helps minimize distractions and excuses. It gives the mind and body an opportunity to remember and feel the excitement, passion, and enthusiasm experienced when the goals were originally set. When you are focused on the what, and the why, the how will take care of itself.

As we have discussed earlier, the mind is very powerful at manifesting and creating opportunities for you to succeed when you are in the right state of mind. Reviewing regularly, promotes the mindset and energy required to stay focused and committed. Reflecting upon where you have come from and the lessons and gifts of your experiences, will assist in avoiding the same mistakes and challenges. As history has a way of repeating itself, without stopping to reflect on the lessons and gifts, more obstacles are bound to arise.

Success lies in a masterful consistency
around the fundamentals.
– Robin Sharma

The following are several Homeplay activities I have used to generate success. It is not necessary to do each one. Choose the one or two processes that resonate with you the most and incorporate that exercise into your life. They will provide the inspiration, motivation, and energetic shift you have been looking for!

Homeplay: Mind Tracker

Time: 30-90 minutes the first time doing the exercise, then 5-10 minutes for each subsequent time.

Purpose: To become aware of where you are on the path to your goal, and make adjustments as needed.

Materials Required: Paper and Pen

Exercise:

This exercise could be done daily, bi-weekly, weekly, monthly, and yearly. It works very well for visual and kinaesthetic learners.

Draw a map, using a large piece of paper. This map is a visual guide to get you from A to Z in relation to your goals. Just like a timeline, begin with a moveable picture of you standing on the left hand side of the paper, with today's date. This represents you setting the goal right now. On the far right hand side of the paper, draw yourself at the finish line, or destination, with your intended date of arrival. Make sure that the destination is enticing and visually pleasing. You want the arrival at your goal to look special and motivating. You can use colours, objects, pictures, magazine prints, etc. In between these two points, you can draw paths, or pencil in possible obstacles that could arise. Labeling deadlines, goal markers, and milestones between these two points, can also be advantageous. As you go through the days, weeks, and months ahead, use the map as a visual guide to lead you toward your goal. Progress the moveable representation/picture of you down the path, adding in obstacles avoided or overcome, success stops, lessons learned, and anything else that represents your journey to success. Every day, spend a couple of minutes focusing on the far right hand side where you have achieved the goal. See and FEEL yourself being successful, and be open to receiving new ideas or strategies that will get you to that place in a more fun and enjoyable way. Each day, move the picture of you in the direction that you feel you are going, based on the action steps taken. As you move, draw the path that you have taken, so you can look back and see your progress, lessons, and successes.

Takeaway:

Visually seeing yourself move towards your goal is very motivating. Taking the time to review consistently, and move the picture of you along the path, allows you the opportunity to reflect on your progress and make corrections. Achieving milestones and short-term goals on the path develops a feeling of accomplishment, which is contagious, creating the desire for more success. Success breeds success.

Homeplay: Inventory

Time: 5+ minutes

Purpose: To become aware of where you are on the path to your goal, and make adjustments as needed.

Materials Required: Paper and Pen

Exercise:

Questions to ask yourself on a daily basis:

Where am I currently in relation to my goal?
What do I need to be, or do, to get closer to my goal today?
Why do I want my goal?
What could get in the way of me being successful?
How can I minimize or prevent these things from happening?
When and how will I celebrate my successes?

Takeaway:

These questions encompass the main focus points when working towards a specific intention. Review where you are now, what you need to do, why you want what you want, what could get in the way with possible solutions, and anticipate planned celebrations for your successes. Focusing on these points daily will remind the conscious mind of your intentions and desires. Where attention goes, energy flows. Keeping your attention on your intensions creates determination. As you already learned, setting a goal with only the conscious mind will not help change behaviours. This process conditions the subconscious mind to get on board with what your conscious mind is telling it. This is a simple but powerful exercise that is best done first thing in the morning.

Homeplay: Journal

Time: 20-45+ minutes

Purpose: To uncover and become aware of your thoughts, emotions, and behaviours surrounding your progress towards your goals.

Materials Required: Paper and Pen

Exercise:

Choose a specific book or journal to write in. Use it for only this exercise, as you will do it every day. It does not matter whether you write first thing in the morning or last thing before bed. Write for at least twenty minutes, uninterrupted. I like to set an intention for journaling before I start writing. It could be about my day, how I feel about my goals, challenges I am facing, etc. Is there something that you would like more clarity about? Your writing does not need to flow or be grammatically correct. As in previous journaling Homeplay exercises, just write whatever comes up in your mind. The more you journal, the easier it will be, and you may find that twenty minutes is not enough. Do not reread what you wrote as you are writing, as this interrupts free flowing thoughts.

Takeaway:

Writing, particularly with paper and pen, puts us into a type of hypnotic trance where deep seeded beliefs and thoughts can surface. You may find that you were not even consciously aware of what you wrote, which is fantastic!

Homeplay: Positive Negative

Time: 10-15 minutes

Purpose: To become aware of what is more attractive and motivating—your current or new behaviours.

Materials Required: Paper and Pen

Exercise:

Divide a piece of paper into four sections. Choose an unsupportive behaviour in which you continuously struggle with changing. In each corresponding section, list several positives and negatives for both your current and possible new behaviour. On the following page is a condensed example of a chart from a client wanting to stop smoking.

Takeaway:

Each of us is motivated either by being pulled towards something or by moving away from something. Why do you

Positives for Continuing to Smoke	Positives for Stopping Smoking
-seems less stressful -its easier -gives me something in common with others	-healthier -live longer -less expensive -save more money -smell better -better immune system -travel long distances without fearing no smoking areas -don't have to go outside to smoke when in hotels -won't have cravings -have more energy -more lung capacity to play sports -better sex drive
Negatives for Continuing to Smoke	Negatives for Stopping Smoking
-coughing -yellow fingers -I smell bad -sick all the time -bad role model for my kids -No money	-I won't go outside to visit with the smoking group -I will have withdrawals -Don't know what to do when I am stressed or triggered

brush your teeth? Is it to have clean white teeth or is it to avoid cavities? If it is to have clean white teeth, you are generally a move towards type person. If it is to avoid cavities and bad breath, you are most likely motivated by moving away from something.

What is more motivating to this client? Since most of his answers are in the positives for stopping smoking, he is likely motivated by being pulled towards something. He will need to focus on all the positives of why he wants his goal rather than why it is bad for him to keep smoking.

Are you a move towards or a move away person? Use this awareness each morning to focus your attention on the reasons for choosing desired behaviours. Apply this information when you feel the temptation to repeat unwanted behaviours. Sometimes all it takes is a simple reminder of the positive and negatives of your choices.

We are what we repeatedly do.
Excellence, therefore, is not an act, but a habit.
– Aristotle

We Interrupt This Programming

Have you ever noticed that you can be thrown off your path to your goal with one small event? Everything is going well—then, wham! It's like something comes over you to sabotage your efforts. Often, watching TV, talking on the phone, driving, a picture, a certain time of day, an old friend, a particular place, sitting on the couch, when you are stressed, mealtime, hanging out with friends, etc., can trigger you and end up throwing you off track. Triggers are not always bad or unsupportive. Sometimes hearing a particular song come on the radio can take you back to an old happy memory, or trigger a particular feeling. Music and smells are the strongest triggers. That is part of the reason why it is harder to just say the alphabet rather than to sing it.

A trigger is simply an event or incident that sets something off. Russian scientist, Ivan Pavlov, is most famous for his experiment involving ringing a bell to make dogs salivate. During his study, he rang a bell then presented meat to dogs and measured the amount they salivated. After a period of time, he only had to ring the bell for the dogs to start salivating, even without the meat present. The bell was now a trigger for the dogs. They were conditioned to salivate when they heard the ringing of the bell. What are you triggered by? What triggers you to behave in a certain way? Does drinking trigger you to smoke? Does stress trigger you to eat? Does your alarm clock ringing trigger you to be grouchy?

Let's use the example of people, who want to lose weight, being triggered. The person eats healthy and follows all their set out goals for the day, then they sit down to relax in the evening in front of the television. We all know what happens next! They start to get the munchies for snacks. Pretty soon, they realize they ate the whole bag of chips, or box of cookies, and have negated all their healthy habits from earlier in the day. For most clients, it does not matter what time of day they sat down to watch television; they would, within minutes, be triggered to eat. Sitting on the couch watching television was a trigger for their mind to send the message that it was time to chow down. To avoid being triggered and shoved off track, there are many techniques available, but, first, it is important to learn why it is we get triggered.

Every decision we make is based on whether we will receive pain or pleasure. This is determined in our mind based on our belief system. The mind's job is to keep us safe and in a state of pleasure. If we have a belief that we are fat or overweight, our mind wants to keep us safe and right by sabotaging any attempts to change this reality. When a person with the belief that they are overweight tries to lose weight, they struggle and feel like any attempt they make is so much work and effort. And it is! The mind is working extra hard to keep you comfortable and ensuring your beliefs are satisfied. Being thin is unfamiliar to them. What is unfamiliar to the mind is uncomfortable and painful. If an overweight person is used to sitting on the couch in the evening, eating snacks, then changing that habit to going for a walk instead, will feel painful and uncomfortable, because the mind is making it that way!

Preparing for triggers is a perfect spot to start. When we are triggered, we need to stop, look at the different options we have, then choose an action step that takes us closer to our goal. Stop, look, choose! Throughout this book, there are many Homeplay exercises that can assist you in minimizing triggers. However, in the heat of the moment, in that split second where you are making a choice whether to make a supportive or unsupportive decision, you need a pattern interrupt.

Pattern interrupts are exactly what the name implies. They interrupt a pattern, either before, or during it taking place. What negative patterns or habits do you have that keep you from accomplishing what you set out to do?

Chains of habit are too light to be felt
until they are too heavy to be broken.
— Warren Buffett

Homeplay: Trigger Interrupt

Time: 10-15 minutes

Purpose: To interrupt negative, unsupportive triggers from sabotaging our efforts.

Materials Required: Pen and Paper

Exercise:

There is an endless list of things that can trigger us to make poor choices. The point of this exercise is to uncover which triggers throw YOU off track. Here is a list of common triggers that my clients have had: alcohol, watching television, going on the computer, driving, socializing with friends, going to work, seeing in-laws, relaxing, bedtime, waking up in the morning, transitioning from one task to another, feeling sad, happy, anxious, etc.

Make a list of things, people, places, etc., that trigger you to choose an unsupportive response. Beside each trigger, brainstorm remedies or pattern interrupts you could use to stop, look, and choose differently than you have in the past.
A common example:

Trigger: Watching television triggers raiding the fridge for snacks.

Brainstorm remedies/pattern interrupts:

- stop watching television
- do something with my hands when I watch television, e.g. knit, paint, sort receipts, fold laundry, do a crossword puzzle
- don't sit on the couch; do yoga, stretch, walk on the treadmill, exercise on the floor
- chew gum
- drink lots of water

Takeaway:

Just like when we are facing our fears, being prepared and planning ahead can stop spiralling, out of control behaviour. Having and practicing a contingency plan for when you are triggered, minimizes the chances that you will be thrown off course.

I suggest using this next Homeplay exercise in conjunction with the one you just completed. They can work beautifully together once you are aware of your triggers.

Homeplay: Asking Questions

Time: 5 minutes

Purpose: To interrupt a non-supportive action and find clarity and guidance on the next step or decision.

Materials Required: None

Exercise:

Occasionally, you are faced with a fork in the road decision. Choosing between listening to the angel or the devil on your shoulder can be confusing. Instead of having an inner battle and weighing the pros and cons of the right move to make, simply consciously question. Stop what you are doing in the moment and ask yourself some objective questions. The following are examples that I have found to be useful. Employ the ones that fit for your situation or adapt them so they do.

- If I wasn't judging myself right now, what else could I be?
- Do my actions match my priorities?
- What choice can I make right now that will get me closer to my goal?
- If I choose this, what will my life be like in the next year, five years, etc.?
- How does it get better than this?
- What else is possible?

- What would it take to have more of this with ease?
- What is the value of choosing this behaviour?
- What am I looking for by doing this habit/behaviour/activity/etc.?
- What awareness am I having that I am not acknowledging?
- What will feel better?
- Does this feel light or heavy? (This does not mean physically, but rather in your body. Imagine walking down a scary, dark back alley by yourself. Do you feel that shift in your body? It feels a bit heavy and restrictive. This is what it means to be heavy. Visualize yourself in the most joyful place you can imagine. Feel how light and free your body is now. That is what light feels like.)

Takeaway:

Asking questions can assist in gaining clarity for the choice you are faced with. Stopping to ask questions, before taking action, minimizes poor decisions, impulsive actions, and, in the end, regrets.

Homeplay: Oh, Snap!

Time: 1-10 seconds throughout the day

Purpose: To interrupt negative, unsupportive triggers from sabotaging our efforts.

Materials Required: Thick elastic band

Exercise:

Note: If physical self-harm is an issue, please do not do this particular Homeplay.

Start by placing the elastic band around your wrist. Commit to having it there for at least the next 30 days. Anytime you have a negative, unsupportive thought, make a negative choice, or have a craving, pull the elastic far away from your wrist and let it go! Oh, snap! This snap should hurt! You don't want to damage your body, by no means, but it should be uncomfortable. Remember the pain/pleasure syndrome. If a negative thought or action is comfortable, there is no reason to change. Make sure that every time you do something that goes against your goal intentions, or you have stinking thinking, you snap the elastic band. This snapping reinforces that action or thought as painful, and your subconscious mind will start deviating to other more comfortable thoughts and actions. Your mind's job is to protect you, so it will keep you away from experiences that are uncomfortable.

The next step is important, so make sure to include it in the process. Once you have snapped the elastic for the negative thought or action, kiss your wrist and say something positive and supportive. I know this may sound a bit strange, but this reinforces the idea that things will get better and that you love yourself.

Do this entire process three more times from the beginning. Snap the elastic for a negative thought or action, then kiss your wrist and say something positive and supportive.

Takeaway:

If a specific negative thought or action is painful, your subconscious mind will keep you from experiencing that repeatedly. Use the elastic band to assist you in stopping, looking, and choosing. Seeing the elastic on your wrist, for at least 30 days, will serve as a reminder that you are willing to be uncomfortable to get the change you desire. Of course, 30 days is a suggested guideline. Use this technique for a time frame that is most helpful for your specific journey.

Gratitude, Recognition and Celebration

Gratitude

Without the love, support and assistance from others, how long would we live? Not long, particularly if that started when we were born. We rely on others for a majority of our day, whether we are conscious of it or not. Think of how many people we need to rely on just to go buy a coffee at our local coffee shop. How many do you think? Three, five, ten, fifty? My guess is close to a hundred, if not more. Just to get the coffee beans to your local store, from half way across the world, takes pickers, managers, truck drivers, machinists, planters, maintenance crews, accountants, border control officers, fuel operators, store owners, storage workers, etc. What if just one of these groups of workers decided to stop being of service. Do you ever stop to be grateful for everything that is in your life? How often are you grateful for all the beautiful and amazing experiences and sights around you? Do you wait until something tragic or amazing happens before you feel grateful? Shifting your perspective, or being present in this moment right now, is often all it takes to be grateful.

When was the last time you were so overwhelmed with so much gratitude you cried? When was the last time you were grateful for your next breath of air? When was the last time you stopped to smell the flowers? I mean this literally and figuratively. Gratitude is a feeling of appreciation and thankfulness, often resulting in an urge to reciprocate positive actions, thoughts, and energy.

Gratitude is one of the greatest states to be in. When you are truly grateful, you can't be angry. When you are truly grateful, you can't be frustrated, annoyed, or sad. A state of gratitude produces happiness and peace. Is that not what we are all striving for in life?

I have heard people say they have nothing to be grateful for because nothing is going 'right' in their life. How is that possible? Some of the poorest people on this earth are the most grateful. They are grateful for every sip of water, every fork full of food, every drop of rain and every ray of sunshine. Impoverished places host some of the happiest and most grateful people.

Feeling gratitude and not expressing it,
is like wrapping a present and not giving it.
– William Ward

I teach my children to reflect on what they are grateful for every night when we eat our dinner, or at bedtime. We each take a turn telling one another what we are grateful for in our lives.

Since starting this ritual, it is often the highlight of my day. Seeing life through the eyes of a child simplifies life. My five year old son always surprises me with what comes out of his mouth. Some days he is grateful to have BBQ sauce for his pork chop, and the next he is grateful to have clean water to drink. My seven year old daughter often overwhelms me with emotion as she tells me she is grateful for her family, a warm house to live in, and having the opportunity to go to school. Whenever they slip into the 'life is not fair' entitlement thinking, we reflect upon what we are grateful for. "What? We have to leave the park already? I wasn't done playing yet!" This is a common argument around our house, or some version of this, depending upon what we are doing. Reminding my children to be grateful for the time they did have, can shift their perspective.

If they are not grateful for what they have, I will sometimes give them the experience of removing the item, or the opportunity to allow them to learn the lesson of gratitude. For example, my children have always had a healthy appetite and have never been picky eaters, thankfully! Upon arriving home from school, without fail, the first question is always, "What are we having for supper?" Grudgingly, my son complains, "We are having asparagus; I don't like asparagus!" After brainstorming ways to make asparagus taste better using cheese, lemon juice, garlic, etc., I remind him to be grateful that he has food to eat and that it is nutritious. We talk about people who don't have anything to eat, or the quality of packaged food some of their classmates eat. We discuss how it effects the way they learn and grow. When I tell them I love them so much that I don't want to hurt them with processed foods and chemicals, they shift from resistance to acceptance. They will often shift their thinking from, "Mom is punishing us with these green sticks that taste gross," to "This will help me be good at school and grow tall like Mom." If they are still ungrateful for their food, or whatever it is, I will simply offer to take it away. Given the choice of having nothing to eat, or eating the asparagus, they quickly shift into being grateful for something to eat. Now, some of you may be thinking that I am hard on my children, and that not everyone likes certain foods. I agree. I would not want to be given the option of having nothing to eat, or eating olives! To relieve this, my son and daughter each get three to five food items that are on their I don't have to eat and mom can't make me list. Whatever food is on their list, they don't have to eat, and I make a point of having an alternative for them, if I choose to cook one of those items. Some days they are simply grateful that they have a list of foods they don't have to eat! Gratitude shifts negative thinking into a more positive perspective and objective reasoning.

Be thankful for what you have; you'll end up having more.
If you concentrate on what you don't have,
you will never, ever have enough.
– Oprah Winfrey

The fastest way to shift out of negative energy and thinking is to be grateful. Trade expectation for appreciation, and watch what shifts happen in your life. The following gratitude Homeplay activities will assist you in getting into this desired state.

Homeplay: Gratitude Challenge

Time: 2 minutes

Purpose: To shift into a state of gratitude.

Materials Required: Paper and Pen

Exercise:

Choose any of the following options to start your gratitude practice. Ideally, do something to BE in a state of gratitude every day.

Option 1: Set the timer for two minutes. Write as many things as you can that you are grateful for. Do this on a weekly basis and challenge yourself to come up with more items each time. The more you do this Homeplay, the easier it is to recognize and appreciate aspects of your life. You can even challenge a friend or spouse to do this with you, for a friendly competition of who can create the longest list!

Option 2: Start with writing down 50 things that you are grateful for. Each week, increase the total number by 10, so, in the second week, you are writing 60 things you are grateful for. You may think 50 is a large number to start with. If you can't come up with 50 things to be grateful for, you really need to do more gratitude exercises!

Option 3: Every day write 10 things that you are grateful for in your life. Do this every day for one week. The challenge is to not write the same thing twice during that week. For example, if you were grateful for a warm house to live in on Monday, you can't write that same gratitude item again until the following Monday. For an extra challenge, see if you cannot repeat any items for an entire month.

Takeaway:

When you challenge yourself to be grateful, you will discover that you seek out and become aware of things, people, and experiences throughout your day that you could use for the Homeplay activities. Gratitude breeds gratitude. The more you are grateful, the more things will come into your life to be grateful for.

Doing these gratitude challenges has a similar experience to buying a new vehicle. Before you bought your new blue van, you never noticed any blue vans on the road, but now you see them everywhere. There are many sayings that speak of this, such as: "What you put your focus on, expands;" "Where attention goes, energy flows;" "You get more of what you focus on." Spend more energy and time on being grateful, and those are the type of experiences you will attract into your life. Being appreciative for each lesson and gift of your journey towards your goal, whether deemed positive or negative, is essential.

As we express our gratitude, we must never forget that the highest appreciation is not to utter words, but to live by them.
– John F. Kennedy

Recognition

Recognition is acknowledging and appreciating forward momentum and achievement. Often, recognition is through formal awards, certificates, trophies, etc. While it can feel great to be recognized by others, we want to focus on internal recognition. External sources are unpredictable, unreliable, subjective, and untimely. Why wish and wait for someone else to provide a reward or feedback. Acknowledging yourself for your efforts, progress, and successes is internally motivating and inspiring. Studies have proven that internal motivation, and rewards, out-perform external by a significant margin. This means you get more payoffs and are more proud of yourself for self-accomplishment than you do when someone else recognizes you.

When was the last time you stopped to recognize and appreciate just how awesome you are? Waiting until you achieve your long-term goal before you recognize your hard work and progress sounds depressing and discouraging. After each milestone, after overcoming a challenge, after making a good decision, and even after taking small steps, acknowledge your efforts and achievements. Recognizing your successes along the way to your goal will keep your enthusiasm and positive mindset in the forefront. The following are ways to acknowledge yourself; choose the one(s) that resonate with you the most and do them as often as possible.

Homeplay: 5 Successes

Time: 5 minutes

Purpose: To recognize your successes, accomplishments and progress, thus increasing motivation and momentum.

Materials Required: Paper and Pen

Exercise:

At the end of every day, write down five ways you were successful at getting closer to your goal. These do not need to be big, huge, giant leaps of success. Depending upon where you are on your journey, something as small as making a phone call to a potential client, walking by the junk food aisle at the grocery store and not buying anything, only having one piece of dessert instead of three, or saying your affirmations that day, could be successful steps.

Alternative: In the morning, write down five steps that you intend to do that day to move you in the direction of your goal. At the end of the day, check off those that you accomplished, and write down any extra or alternative ones you did as well.

Takeaway:

Success breeds success. When we see ourselves as successful, it is contagious, and we strive for more. Being successful raises our self-esteem and self-confidence as well. Feeling good about yourself will expand your energy and positive mindset, making it easier to achieve your goal.

The more you praise and celebrate your life,
the more there is in life to celebrate.
– Oprah Winfrey

Celebration

Celebrating is the most overlooked and underestimated ingredient in creating goals. It is very similar to recognition. Recognition is more of an internal acknowledgement, while celebration is an external, "Whoot whoot!" Waiting until the finish line to celebrate doesn't make sense. Celebrating increases motivation, inspiration, self-esteem, self-confidence, as well as feelings of pride, happiness, and joy. Could you use more of these things to launch you to your goal? Make celebration a part of your journey with the following Homeplay activities.

Homeplay: Party Hat

Time: Will vary. 5 minutes-3+ hours

Purpose: To celebrate your success, progress, and achievements thus far, which will increase motivation, focus, and positive energy.

Materials Required: Will vary. Big milestones or successes must include at least one other person.

Exercise:

In Chapter 2, you completed a Homeplay called Ready, Set, Chunk! Go back to this activity and mark in times WHEN you will celebrate and HOW you will celebrate. At least once per month, plan to have a significant festivity, with smaller celebrations scattered throughout the weeks.

As you move along your path to your goal, celebrate and share your successes with at least one other person. Depending on the size of your accomplishment, this could look like phoning up a friend or your accountability buddy to share what you have accomplished, doing something special that you don't normally do, or throwing a party with cake and party hats. Whatever it is that you do to celebrate, make it meaningful and fun!

Ideas for celebrating: Going out to a movie with a friend, signing up for a class, getting a make- over, hiring someone to clean your house, making a certificate of achievement on your computer, taking a picture of yourself by a milestone, having a dance party by yourself or with your family in your living room, hanging a congratulations banner and sitting with a cup of tea, going out dancing with your friends, having friends over for a game night, going on a trip or vacation, going to a comedy club, taking a day off work, sitting and feeling proud of yourself for a few minutes, going bowling, karaoking with friends, doing something off your bucket list, sending the kids to their grandparents for the night for some alone time with a spouse, buying a new outfit, going out for supper, going for a walk in nature, getting a massage, etc.

Takeaway:

Making celebration part of the process reignites the fire of desire and determination. Plus, it provides an opportunity for you to step back from the nose in the dirt work to have fun and relax. Don't wait until you have achieved your long-term goal before celebrating.

The secret of change is to focus all of your energy, not on fighting the old, but on building the new.
– Socrates

Chapter 5: Key Concepts

- When you are focused on the what and the why, the how will take care of itself.
- Reviewing your goals and the reasons you want those goals, on a daily basis, helps minimize distractions and excuses.
- Where attention goes, energy flows.
- Writing, particularly with paper and pen, puts us into a type of hypnotic trance where deep seeded beliefs and thoughts can surface.
- Each of us is motivated either by being pulled towards something or by moving away from something.
- Every decision we make is based on our belief system determining whether we will receive pain or pleasure. The mind's job is to keep us safe and in a state of pleasure.
- What is unfamiliar to the mind is uncomfortable and painful.
- Gratitude is one of the greatest states to be in.
- The fastest way to shift out of negative energy and thinking is to be grateful.
- Trade expectation for appreciation.
- Gratitude breeds gratitude. The more you are grateful, the more things will come into your life to be grateful for.
- Recognizing your successes along the way to your goal will keep your enthusiasm and positive mindset in the forefront.
- Success breeds success. When we see ourselves as successful, it is contagious, and we strive for more.
- Making celebration part of the process reignites the fire of desire and determination.

Chapter 6

Rest and Rejuvenate:
Powering Up and Down

When climbing a mountain, do hikers start at the bottom and continuously walk up to the top? Do formula one drivers complete the entire race without stopping? Will you make forward progress consistently towards your goal? No, of course not! Thinking this way is detrimental and faulty. There is no straight path to a goal.

When mountain climbers aim to reach the top, they plan out several rest stops along the way. Climbers plan for when they may need to push through obstacles, and for periods where they can take their time. Sometimes they push themselves too hard at the beginning and burn out. If this happens, they need to go back to the bottom and try again another time. If you focus only on your goal and ignore other areas of your life, you will burn out and be unhappy. Focus and determination can be strengths and weaknesses. Coming out of the starting gate full force will often lead to wearing yourself out physically, emotionally, and spiritually. Burnout requires restarting, often at where you began. Learn to pace yourself. Knowing when to put in late nights, and when to take a day off, can be the difference between success and setback.

Sometimes climbers feel great and make great progress, leading them to want to continue past the planned upon rest stop. Pushing past a place where you know you need to stop and rest can be disadvantageous. Being overtired, stressed, or under pressure, incapacitates smart decision making. Climbers who push past rest stops usually find themselves backtracking down the mountain to get the required rest and rejuvenation they needed. Thinking you are making progress by sacrificing your sleep, relationships, or finances, can only result in backtracking. Backtracking brings feelings of discouragement, failure, unworthiness, and hopelessness, and lowers self-esteem and self-confidence. To avoid this from happening to you, apply the lessons in this chapter.

With carefully planned out stops to rest and rejuvenate, the journey to your goal will seem easier than you thought possible. It is only when you don't use the tools and techniques available that reaching the summit seems difficult or impossible. Climbers would never avoid taking water with them because it slowed them down. They would never wear flip flops because hiking boots are too hot. They use these tools because they were recommended by others before them. These tools have been successfully tried and tested, leading to improved performance and enjoyment. Use the tools and techniques in this book because they too have been successfully tried and tested, resulting in improved performance and enjoyment.

Resting involves more than kicking your feet up at the end of the day or getting the recommended seven to eight hours of sleep per night. It is learning how to power down physically, intellectually, and emotionally. Have you ever had the experience of tossing and turning at night, unable to fall asleep? Do you find when it is time to relax at the end of the day, your mind is still in overdrive? The Homeplay exercises in this chapter will assist you in creating power down habits that have you drifting off to sleep when your head hits the pillow.

Rejuvenating, conversely, is about powering up. It is about feeling juiced, ready, and alive. Are there times when you have felt drained, uninterested, or unenthusiastic when you needed to be turned on? I am not referring to the bedroom, although the exercises in this chapter on rejuvenation did assist one of my clients to trade in her standby headache excuse for more fun between the sheets. Life requires you to shift into being at your 'A' game when you would rather be 'Z'ing on the couch. Learning how to rejuvenate yourself regularly, and at a moment's notice, is key to getting the sale, presenting your best self to a client, getting to the gym, making healthy meals instead of processed ones, or putting on a smile when the in-laws arrive.

Powering up and powering down, when you choose to, decreases wasted time, wasted energy, and wasted money. For some of you reading this book, this is the chapter that will be a game changer. Learning how to turn off your mind at the end of the day to get the required rest you need, how to recharge your batteries, how to avoid energy drains, and how to properly power up, is the difference between having powerful momentum and being powerfully stuck.

Let's Get Physical

The health of your physical body obviously plays a huge part in what you are capable of accomplishing. Without proper nutrition, exercise and rest, your body will physically begin shutting down and not working optimally. To reach your goal, you are going to need stamina, yes? You are going to need perseverance, yes? You are going to need energy, yes? Will a body that is not working at its potential, hinder your progress? Of course! Whether your goal is a physical feat or something done on a screen, you will need your physical body on your side to get you through the tasks ahead. Numerous studies have shown, time and again, that what we eat affects how we think and feel. I am not about to go into a rant about GMOs and processed foods, as there is plenty of information on this subject. At the end of this book, I have listed some resources I recommend if you are interested in examining this further. It is my intention, however, to get you to connect what you are putting into your body, and how you are moving your body, with your ability to reach your goal.

It is near impossible to power up to 100% when your body is fighting to rid itself of chemicals, toxins, and dehydration.

Homeplay: Drink Up Buttercup!

Time: 1-2 minutes, several times a day

Purpose: Power up by hydrating your body, so it can function effectively with increased energy.

Materials Required: Water.

Exercise:

Take your weight and divide it by two. This is how many ounces of water is suggested you drink every day. Let me state that again. This is how much WATER to drink—not tea, coffee, pop, or juice. For example, if you weigh 160 pounds, you will need to drink about 80 ounces of water every day. This is approximately 10 cups. If you are physically active, you will probably need to drink more.

Drink this amount of water every day for the next 21 days. If you don't drink any water right now, start off slowly. Start with drinking half of the recommendation, and increase the amount every day for the next week. You will probably notice you require bathroom breaks more often. Do not let this deter you from drinking more! I have found that the body will adjust after the first few days, reducing the number of potty dances.

Hints: From my experience, it can appear overwhelming to drink this much water in one day when you are first starting out. The following are hints to assist you in drinking the recommended amount of water your body needs.

- Drink a big glass when you first wake up in the morning. This will kick your metabolism into gear and help flush out unwanted toxins.
- Add fresh lemon juice or slices to your water to improve its taste.
- Get a quality filter to ensure the water you are drinking tastes good and is good for you.

- At least half an hour before you eat, drink a big glass of water. There are three glasses of water right there!
- Set a timer on your phone for every 30 minutes to an hour, to serve as a reminder to drink a glass of water.
- Drink most, or all, of your water before dinner, so you don't need to get up in the night to go to the bathroom.
- Space your glasses of water out throughout your day. Ensure you are not fulfilling your quota solely in the evening resulting in floating and swishing your way into bed.
- Exercise! Moving your body will increase your desire to drink water. What a great way to check off two things at once!
- Create a checklist for every glass of water you drink, you can even put a checkmark or a sticker on afterward.
- Make a water challenge with your family or co-workers to keep you motivated.
- Set up a reward or incentive for yourself, such as "I only get coffee tomorrow morning if I reach my water intake today."

Takeaway:

Most people are walking around with low energy because they are dehydrated. Dehydration can cause headaches, dry skin, dry mouth, sleepiness, and constipation. When dehydrated, our bodies are not able to function properly. Water equals energy. A guideline to assist you in determining if you are dehydrated or not is to look at your urine. If it is light or dark yellow, then you are most likely dehydrated. Some supplements make this test invalid as they turn your urine yellow. Energy drinks, while giving the illusion of increased energy, merely supply a spike in insulin and result in a crash. They are harmful for your body, as your body needs to work harder to get rid of the high amounts of caffeine and sugar contained in these drinks. They may appear helpful short term but will put you further behind in the long run. Stay powered up with clean natural water!

Other recommended physically healthy habits to incorporate into your life that will improve your rate of success are: getting between seven to nine hours of sleep every night, having consistent sleep and wake times every day, moving your body 30 minutes every day with three times a week moderate to strenuous activities, eat foods that have less than five ingredients on the label, eat foods that only have ingredients you can pronounce and recognize, eat at least seven to ten fruits and vegetables every day, eliminate GMO food products, grow your own garden, buy organic, use a water filter in your shower, drink filtered water, and use alternative medicines and therapies.

Shhh! It's Quiet Time

Quiet time can be sleeping, meditating, journaling, resting your body and mind, or just unplugging from the constant noise and distractions. Being plugged in, and pulled in so many different directions, disperses and ultimately drains your energy. When your mind is overloaded with information, it will physically start shutting your body down to prepare you for sleep. It does this so your conscious mind can process information and download the pertinent messages into your subconscious mind for storage. Basically, it needs time to sort and file. Have you ever noticed your energy deplete when you are studying to retain facts, listening to a lecture, or preparing taxes for the year? It is your brain being overloaded and needing time to filter the information.

Years ago, there were not the extra pressures and stresses like there are today. I see this particularly with families that have children. Many families now have two working parents and drive their children every night of the week, and most weekends, to activities. When do these families have time to power down? Being revved up all day and rushing to the next activity takes a toll, not only on physical health, but mental as well. Eventually, in these types of situations, people begin to run on adrenaline and artificial supplements like energy drinks. These short-term solutions not only disrupt the natural flows and systems in the body, but also fool you into believing that you don't need to listen to your body. Listening to your body is a skill for connecting with your intuition and following those gut instincts. It will guide you in making decisions, so the inner conflict of making the 'right' choice is minimized. When faced with a choice, your gut instinct or intuition will tell you, but you have to be open to listen. Have you ever had a gut feeling and didn't listen? What was the result?

I never used to listen to my body, and it is still something I continue to work on. I lived my days in my head, thinking that this was what ran the show. It wasn't until I got engaged that my gut feelings started to become apparent. In fact, the closer the wedding date, the louder and more clear the message. There were many times, over the year engagement, that I had overwhelming doubt and resistance show up. This was not just regular cold feet; this was based on solid facts that kept accumulating. Had I stopped to listen and check in with how I was feeling, my life events would have turned out much differently. Your body will tell you how you feel about something before your mind has a chance to analyze it, put it through belief systems, and create thoughts about it. By stopping and being still, we can listen to the body give us answers by how it reacts and feels. Often, people get some of their most brilliant ideas in the shower, because, during that time, the distractions of life are minimal, and they are grounded into their bodies. The feel of the water on their skin gets them out of their heads and into their bodies, allowing creativity to flow unobstructed. So, besides wasting water standing in a shower or sitting staring at the wall, what can you do to create stillness and peace in your life, while taking time to power down or power up? The following Homeplay activities will give you some ideas.

Homeplay: Deep Breathing and Body Talk

Time: 10-15 minutes

Purpose: To slip away from the busyness of life and connect with how your body is feeling. Some people call this connecting with your intuition. Being connected with your intuition, or higher self, allows you to more confidently make decisions and take action steps, which are in alignment with your deepest values. When listening to this part, the F.E.A.R (false evidence appearing real) is not taken into account. The practice of being still and quiet allows the body to recover from stress and its side effects.

Materials Required: None

Exercise:

1. Start by finding a quiet space where no one will disturb you. Shut off your phone. No, don't just set it to vibrate, as that will just distract you. The idea is to be distraction free for the next ten minutes or more.

2. Next, focus on your breathing. When someone first told me to focus on my breath, I thought, "Alright with the fluffy stuff. Just get to the punch line." For those of you who struggle to be still and quiet for any length of time, I suggest you do this more often, for a shorter period of time, until your body gets accustomed! You are not looking at fulfilling a time quota by letting your mind wander. Short and sweet is better than long and lazy. When someone says, "Focus on your breath," often that happens for about one inhale and exhale; then your mind takes you off on a tangent. There are many different ways to focus on your breathing, such as counting your breaths, saying a mantra or affirmation with each breath, repeating a power word, etc. You choose which is best for you! You are not striving for cross-legged, levitating yogi here. Perfection and pose will not give you extra points. Breathing deeply increases the oxygen to your brain and relaxes your nervous system. It assists in taking you out of the fight or flight response and running on adrenaline that can be caused by too much stress and burnout. It is an easy practice that you can do anywhere, anytime, in as little as 10 seconds to help relax and clear your mind. As you do this throughout your day, while waiting at the doctor's office, stuck in traffic jams, cooking supper, etc., notice if you are holding your breath, or breathing very shallow before you started.

As an aside, if you decide to do deep breathing while standing in line somewhere, make sure to do it as quietly as possible. I came to this realization after practicing my deep breathing while in line at the grocery store. The innocent elderly lady in front of me gave me a dirty look while stating irritatedly, "I am going as fast as I can." I felt horrible at the misunderstanding but was able to laugh with her after explaining what I was actually doing!

If you are unfamiliar with deep breathing or belly breathing, the following are a few techniques that can get you started. Beginners should start off very slow, as the increase of oxygen can make you feel dizzy or give you a slight headache. Always breathe in through your nose and out through your mouth. When you breathe in, your belly should push out, and when you breathe out, your belly should push in. If you get confused, just think of trying to blow out a cake full of candles. When blowing out air, you need your belly to come in and up to push all the air out of your lungs. It is not necessary, while deep breathing, to puff up your chest like a cartoon character; just a full, natural breath is all you need.

Technique 1: Re-lax Breath
Think of the word relax. It has two syllables, re and lax. As you take a deep breath in, think re to yourself, and as you breathe out completely, think lax. It is not necessary to say the word out loud when you breathe, just think it in your mind. Relax. When you breathe out, imagine and feel yourself letting go of any tensions or stress in your body. The out-breath is the one to focus on, as the in-breath takes care of itself!

Technique 2: Breath Counting
Take a deep breath in, then on the exhale, count 1. Only on the exhaling breaths, will you count. On the next exhaling breath, you will count 2. Continue to breathe deeply until you get to 5 exhales. Then start back at 1 again.

Technique 3: 7777 (Advanced)
Breathe in deeply and slowly to the count of 7, then hold that breath for a count of 7. Exhale through your nose, slowly, to a count of 7, then hold your breath for a count of 7. Repeat. Can

you guess how many times? That's right— 7!

These are only three easy ways to get you going, there are countless methods to help focus your mind on your breath. Start with breathing for 10-30 seconds to begin with, several times a day. If you are a seasoned belly breather, feel free to do longer sessions. Setting an alarm on your phone can remind you to take a few deep breaths throughout your day. Likewise, developing the habit of taking some deep breaths at certain times of the day can be helpful; for instance, before eating meals, before answering the phone, while washing your hands, or even while making a trip to the washroom. Some trips, I suppose, already take care of the deep breathing—but you get the idea.

3. As you develop a practice of deep breathing, you will find your body naturally relaxes quickly after only a few breaths. After just three conscious deep breaths, my body is conditioned to feel as relaxed as I do before I fall asleep at night. Pretty handy for stressful situations! After getting into a relaxed state, you can choose to continue just watching your breath go in and out, and see what sensations or thoughts arise, or you can open up to a question you may be pondering on.

4. If you are choosing to ask a question, simply think of the question in your mind. Do not try looking for an answer; just imagine it floating out into the universe, and trust the answer will show up when and how it needs to. Basically, don't be attached to getting an answer back on your time schedule. After sending the question, focus on your breathing and sensations in your body once again.

If you did not ask a question, you will simply observe your breath and sensations in your body. Feel the breath coming in through your nose. Does it tickle? What does it feel like in your body to pause between breaths? Does it feel relieving to breathe in again after an exhale? Focus on the sensations in your body. Where are you tense in your body? Imagine sending your inhaling breath to that part that feels tense. Is your stomach in a knot? Do your legs feel heavy? What does the chair feel like underneath you? Continue to be passively curious of the sensations in your body and of inner dialogue. If you find your mind wandering off to other things that are unsupportive to you in this moment, just imagine putting that thought onto a cloud and watch it float out of sight. When it is out of sight, you will be able to focus on the sensations in your body.

5. Be open and aware of any sensations or inner dialogue that can support you in taking the next step, providing answers to your questions, or giving you insight. Regardless, if you gain any new awareness, the practice of disconnecting from life in a healthy way will allow you to be more focused and productive. No making excuses that you don't have time to do this! Stopping to get grounded and clear can save you hours, days, weeks, and sometimes years, of anguish and frustration.

Takeaway:

While in a relaxed state, creative juices flow easier and are unrestricted. With the nervous system at ease, the body has an opportunity to function more efficiently and effectively. No one enjoys feeling stressed, anxious, or exhausted. Trying to work towards goals when you are always feeling drained and worn out, will never last. Deep breathing will increase the oxygen in your body, increase circulation, reduce stress and its side effects, and will energize you! Did I mention there are no downsides to this?!?

Once relaxed with an increased level of oxygen, it will be easier to follow those gut instincts that point you in the right direction. Listening to your body and allowing it the opportunity to send you messages will assist you in feeling energized and confident that you are on the right path to your goal.

At my children's school, they teach deep breathing as a stress release and calming down tool. My son, while he was in kindergarten, enjoyed doing yoga in his classroom and learning to 'breathe big'. I thought it was cute, but I didn't really believe that he would implement the technique unless reminded. Much to my surprise, a few months later, he stopped to take a few deep breaths to calm himself down before swinging his golf club at a ball he had grown increasingly frustrated with! If he can do it, you can too! Those few short seconds he took to stop and breathe, helped him crack the ball into the air, which was an improvement to only grass flying before.

The deep breathing exercises can assist you throughout the day to de-stress and be present in your body. Practicing this throughout the day will improve your ability to fall asleep at night, as you will have already processed a lot of your day. Often, people have difficulty powering down at the end of the day because they are bombarded with so much stimuli from the time they wake up until the time they go to sleep. Their bodies are conditioned to be ON all the time. Our mind requires time to process, download and expel information, before we lay our heads on the pillow. If we don't have a powering down routine before we intend to fall asleep, it is common to toss and turn with thoughts from the day keeping you awake.

Electronic devices, used before bedtime, mess with circadian rhythms, tricking our brains into thinking it is daytime, not night time. Screen time before bed promotes wakefulness, making it difficult to fall asleep. Do you look at a screen from a tablet, television, computer, or phone, before bed? Or, even worse, in bed?! If you are having trouble falling asleep at night, this is the first routine to break! Allowing an hour or two between screen time and pillow time will improve your quality of sleep.

After high school, I took a year to work and gain experience in the real world. I had the opportunity to work at my uncle's accounting office for the tax season, helping with organizing and recording receipts, among other things. At the end of the day, I remember feeling so drained and tired, even though I had sat behind a desk all day. I often struggled to fall asleep at night and resorted to watching television late at night. I felt exhausted, but I couldn't fall asleep. For the three months I worked there, it felt like I could never get rested or get a good quality sleep. My mind was switched to ON all the time, and I didn't have the tools and techniques to find the OFF switch. Fortunately, I never have the problem of tossing and turning, or my mind racing, preventing me from sleeping anymore. When I put my head on the pillow, and I am ready to sleep, I... am... out like a light!

Homeplay: Unplug Yourself

Time: 1 minute

Purpose: To get a better quality of sleep in order to feel rested, refreshed, and rejuvenated.

Materials Required: None

Exercise:

1. Shut off all screens for a minimum of one hour before you go to sleep.

2. Choose an activity for the last hour before you go to sleep, to prepare you for the deep slumber to come—any activity that begins to power your brain off from thinking, analyzing, or taking in information. Also, avoid any activity that is physically active. This means if you want a quality sleep, you should not be squeezing in a late night 5 mile run. Activities that provide peacefulness, relaxation, and comfort could include reading (books that are non-violent or intellectually thought provoking), knitting, taking a hot bath, meditating, deep breathing, painting, stretching, journaling, planning out the next day (only if this feels relaxing and comforting), preparing for the next day, writing in a gratitude journal, listing successes for the day, etc.

Takeaway:

Power down the electronics, so you can power down too! The blue light from screens keeps your brain turned ON, even if you are wanting to power down for the night. Checking social media, as a relaxing activity while in bed, is not a good option if quality 'Zzz' is what you are expecting when you shut off the lights. Even if you fall asleep quickly, the stimulation from screens disrupts the deep sleep patterns for you to get a restful slumber. There are apps and special glasses that can minimize this effect if turning off the screen is unthinkable. Remember, you can have the reasons, or you can have the results. Excuses don't get results.

These previous Homeplay activities aimed to assist you in powering down, so your body and mind can rejuvenate. The next Homeplay is geared to power you up and get your passion flowing. This is a good activity to use in the morning to set your energy for the day.

Homeplay: Islands of Success

Time: 5 minutes

Purpose: To shift into the energy required to naturally move you towards your goals.

Materials Required: 3 full sheets of paper

Exercise:

1. Label sheet number one with the words, Past Positive Experience. Label the second sheet, Positive Feelings, and label the third sheet, My Goal. On the second sheet, Positive Feelings, choose 3–5 powerful feelings that would help propel you to your goal. If you felt this way, reaching your goal would be easy and fun, e.g., motivated, confident, persistent, joyful, patient, grounded, inspired, tenacious, etc.

2. Spread the sheets out on the floor in front of you.

3. In a moment, you are going to stand on each sheet separately. While standing on the second sheet, Positive Feelings, choose one feeling that you wrote down to focus on. Take a few moments to really feel that feeling in your body. What is your posture like when you feel this way? Are your shoulders down and back? Are you smiling or content? Are you tense or relaxed?

4. Once you experience this feeling in your body, move to stand on the first piece of paper, Past Positive Experience. Imagine, visualize, and experience yourself in the past when you felt that feeling from the second sheet. This could be any experience you had that made you feel that particular positive feeling. Take a few moments to remember the details and how it felt in your body.

5. Step back onto sheet number two, Positive Feelings, and choose the next powerful feeling word. Take a few moments to feel what that word feels like in your body.

6. Move back to sheet number one, Past Positive Experience. Spend some time visualizing or imagining a situation in your past where you felt this feeling.

7. Continue to do this back and forth pattern between the two sheets until you have gone through each of the power words.

8. Once you have finished each of the power words, you will feel amazing! Next, step onto sheet number three, My Goal.

With the feelings of all your positive, powerful words flowing through you, anchor that feeling into your goal. To do this, place your thumb and forefinger together and visualize yourself successfully achieving all the action steps to your goal, and actually reaching your goal. It is important to feel all your positive, powerful feelings while doing this anchoring exercise.

9. Release your fingers and step off of the sheet feeling empowered!

Takeaway:

Anytime you need to feel your positive, powerful feelings, just place your thumb and forefinger together and take a deep breath. The more you repeat this Homeplay exercise, the faster and stronger the feelings will come to you when you fire your anchor of placing your thumb and forefinger together. Feeling motivated, empowered, patient, and confident are simply states of mind and energy that you can shift into anytime it is required. Having the ability to shift your energy into these positive states on demand is useful to keep you focused, on track, and making forward progress. Who couldn't use more of that? Powering up is at your fingertips—literally!

Everything is energy and that's all there is to it.
Match the frequency of the reality you want and you
cannot help but get that reality. It can be no other way.
This is not philosophy. This is physics.
– Albert Einstein

The Forbidden 'F' Word

When on a mission, and set on a goal, how does one usually behave?—Serious, focused, reacts grumpily at distractions, even well-meaning ones. While at times being serious, focused on the task at hand, and concentrating, is essential; it can also be draining if done for too long. Life is too short to not have fun! Fun is what keeps our energy up and our outlook optimistic. Have you ever had the experience of not really feeling like going out with your friends because you were too tired or had a long day? If you decided to go out anyway, and chose to have FUN, I am guessing an abundance of energy appeared as if from nowhere! The energy that is created through enjoying life will transfer to you as you embark on action steps to your goal. As we have discussed before, relaxing allows creativity to flow, and your nervous system to recharge. Having fun is the most joyful way to productively relax! The forbidden 'F' word, if you haven't guessed it already, is Fun.

During my first year of university, I was repeatedly told by my parents that I needed to go out and have some fun. I know, I wasn't the typical student. My mother even sent me gift certificates to a local sports bar to encourage me to get out of my room for a few hours. I hoarded them and never felt like I had time for fun. I, unlike most of my dorm mates, spent sunup to sundown, and long after that, studying for my classes. I took meticulous notes during class, then came back to my room to rewrite them. From there, I would then condense the notes even further to just the main points, highlighting, colour coding, etc. I was the epitome of a nerd, just without the high marks to show for my efforts. While most of my classmates were out having fun, I was the grumpy one on the floor telling everyone to be quiet so I could do my assigned reading. I thought that the harder I worked, the better marks I would achieve. It took me three years to realize that it doesn't actually work that way. I grew resentful and frustrated that I was struggling, while my partying friends (who didn't even buy the textbook) were doing well in their classes. What was I doing wrong? My brain was working so hard that it couldn't absorb everything I was throwing at it. It stopped retaining information well before I decided it was time to quit. I remember reading pages of textbooks two or three times because I would get to the bottom of the page, or to the end of the chapter, and couldn't tell you one thing I learned. During my fourth and fifth years of university, I had a roommate that made me go out to have fun. It was hard to understand how I could do less school work and get better marks, but it was the way it was! Fun fixed everything!

> *People rarely succeed unless they have*
> *fun in what they are doing.*
> – Dale Carnegie

Homeplay: Finding Your Fun

Time: 15-30+ minutes

Purpose: To rejuvenate and recharge your energy through the act of having fun. Fun is defined as the act of lightheartedness, enjoyment, or amusement.

Materials Required: Paper and Pen

Exercise:

1. Brainstorm, research, or get support in creating a list of things that you have fun doing. I encourage you to choose things that do not involve zoning out in front of an electronic screen. You will know the activity is fun if you feel lighthearted and carefree, almost as though you were a kid again.

For you Type A readers, this list can be categorized into different areas such as: activities that cost money, activities that are free, activities that take less than thirty minutes, activities that take over two hours, activities that require someone else, activities that can be done at home, etc. I realize that, for those of you who do not know what you enjoy doing, this task may seem overwhelming or daunting. It did for me when I tried doing it many years ago. What I enjoy doing, sadly seemed like one of the toughest questions I ever had to answer! Below are some helpful hints that will get you started. Naturally, add to your list as ideas present themselves.

2. Commit to doing something that is fun every day. Yes, every day! I am not suggesting you need to take half a day off work every day to go skydiving if that is your twisted idea of what you think is fun. It could be something as simple as doing a cartwheel in the backyard, jumping in a mud puddle, playing with children, or dancing to your favourite song like no one is watching. At least once a month, commit to one larger activity that is fun. This could be having a games night with friends, sleeping in the backyard in a tent, going mini golfing or making a craft— anything that may take a longer period of time that cannot be done on a daily basis.

Takeaway:

Incorporating fun activities into your daily routine will shift your energy into a positive enthusiastic state. Positive energy equals productivity and progress. Your goal is only part of the picture, enjoying the ride is what will get you there.

Life is not a destination, it is a journey.
– Ralph Waldo Emerson

Homeplay: Laughter Yoga

Time: 5-30+ minutes

Purpose: To rejuvenate and recharge your energy through the act of having fun. Fun is defined as the act of lightheartedness, enjoyment or amusement.

Materials Required: Paper and Pen

Exercise:

I ensure that at least one of my daily fun activities for the week involves laughing. I was introduced to laughter yoga at a cancer convention that our town hosted. It not only lifted everyone's spirits to recharge their energy, it was a good work out! The part I loved about the session was no one had to tell jokes or do something to make me laugh. All we did was start pretending to laugh. This continued for only a few seconds before real laughter broke out and everyone was holding their bellies! Fake laughter turns into real laughter, and laughter is contagious. There are many videos online that can support you in getting started. I often start by simply listening to other people laugh, which gets me giggling, and, in no time, gasping for air to catch my breath. Doing this with a group of people is ideal. Even just thinking about laughter sessions provokes me to start smiling.

Takeaway:

Laughter increases the oxygen in your body just like deep breathing does. It also gets the feel good endorphins flowing, which naturally improves your mood. The effects of laughing last far longer than when it is done. It is about the easiest, quickest, and most fun way to shift into a positive energetic state. Power up with perpetual laughter!

Getting Out of the Zone

The idea of having fun leads us to our next topic of Getting Out of the Comfort Zone. Earlier, I mentioned the idea of a comfort zone. A comfort zone is simply what most people cling to. It is the space in which we live that feels safe and secure. I am not specifically referring to physical space, but mental space too. For most people, sitting on the couch watching television in their home, is within their physical comfort zone. Only talking to people you know, when you go to a party, may be in your mental comfort zone. Your body and mind feel safe and secure staying within what you know and what is familiar, thus it is relaxed. The mind's job is to keep you safe. When you go outside of your perceived comfort zone, physical discomfort shows up as anxiety, increased heart rate, sweating, rapid breathing, inability to focus, etc.

If you were to present a speech to an auditorium of 5000 people, would that be in your comfort zone? Most people would have some form of initial resistance to doing this because it is not familiar to them. Not familiar equals unsafe, to the mind. Your mind will start coming up with all the things that could go wrong, or what if situations. What if I trip and fall? What if I lose my place and can't remember what to say? What if everyone laughs at me?

You could live your entire life saying what if, and never do anything uncomfortable, never take any risks, and never live an extraordinary life. My question to you is, "What if you lived inside your comfort zone your entire life because you let fear stand in the way of what you really wanted? What if, on your death bed, you regret not having taken the chance?" Is it worth it to not take a chance?

> *Life begins at the end of your comfort zone.*
> – Neale Donald Walsch

You will need to take risks and be uncomfortable in order to reach your goal. Risks do not need to be physical; they can be emotional or spiritual as well. The more you take small steps outside your comfort zone, the easier it will become. Think of your comfort zone as having a bubble around you. You can stretch the bubble a little bit and it will not pop. It won't be scary or feel too uncomfortable to take small steps. If you try taking too big a leap, the bubble will burst, leaving you to feel very exposed and vulnerable. This can have the potential to be absolutely life-changing but should only be done in a safe space with trained facilitators and support.

Focus on taking steps to consciously get out of habitual patterns that are familiar and comfortable. This could include starting to take a different route to work every day, brushing your teeth with the opposite hand, sleeping on the other side of the bed for awhile, moving furniture around in your house, etc.

Just like an elastic band, stretching your comfort zone slowly and steadily will increase its size. An elastic band or comfort zone, once stretched, will never go back to its original size. It is forever expanded to encompass a larger diameter, which means you will be able to comfortably do more things without your mind feeling fearful. What action step to your goal feels out of your comfort zone right now? Is it asking for a raise, getting into a swimsuit, asking for support, leaving a relationship, or maybe sharing your goal with others? Whatever it is that has you feeling uncomfortable, will not be an issue when you consistently apply the following Homeplay activity.

> *A ship in a harbour is safe,*
> *but that's not what a ship is built for.*
> – Unknown

Homeplay: Stretching the Zone

Time: Will Vary

Purpose: To get comfortable with being uncomfortable, so it will be easier to take risks and unfamiliar steps towards your goal without sabotage or resistance taking over.

Materials Required: Paper and Pen

Exercise:

At least once a week, do something that pushes you out of your comfort zone. Ideally, do something every day. Plan and mark these out on your calendar, so you know the task will get done. The following are some example activities to get you out of your comfort zone. Note: Everyone has a different size of zone to start with, so some of these activities may not feel like a stretch to you, and some may feel like too big of a stretch. How do you know which ones are going to stretch you and not metaphorically pop your comfort zone bubble? Stretching should provoke a bit of fear, uncomfortableness, or anxiety. It should not keep you up at night or have you scrambling to fill a Xanax or Valium prescription.

Examples:

- For ladies with body image issues: wearing a two-piece bathing suit to the beach or pool, going uptown without makeup or your hair done, wearing a sleeveless top, wearing shorts, wearing high heels, wearing lingerie, doing a strip show for your spouse/boyfriend, dancing naked, standing naked in front of the mirror, etc.

- Physical — bungee jumping, rock climbing, bike riding, repelling, zip lining, running, climbing a ladder, looking over a balcony railing, going on a waterslide, riding a rollercoaster, riding a horse, driving a vehicle, getting a completely different haircut, shaving your facial hair or growing it out, holding a snake or spider, sleeping in a tent outside, etc.

- Mental – ask for forgiveness, have a tough conversation with someone, ask for a raise, stand up for yourself, ask for what you want, use no technology for an entire day, sign up for a new class, learn a new language, go on a blind date, fold your hands with the opposite thumb on top, cross your arms the opposite way, etc.

- Face any fear you have!

Hint: Being nervous before stepping outside, or pushing the confines of your comfort bubble, is natural. But are you really nervous, or are you just excited? Nervousness and excitement show up in your body the exact same way: increased heart rate, sweaty hands, faster breathing, etc. The only difference between feeling nervous and excited is how you decide to label those reactions in your body. So, instead of saying, "I am nervous," change it to, "I am excited!" With your mind thinking you are excited, it feels more positive and enticing to do the activity.

Takeaway:

Be open to opportunities presenting themselves. The more you naturally feel comfortable stretching outside of your comfort zone, the more successful you will be. Your mind will be conditioned to not let unfamiliar situations stop you from pushing through. If you don't learn how to feel this discomfort long enough to learn the new behaviour, new thoughts, and new emotions, you will stay stuck. Short-term discomfort for long-term gain—until your brain feels safe pushing the walls of your comfort zone. With this new way of thinking, obstacles will just be something you navigate around instead of allowing them to stop you. Once you have stretched your comfort bubble, it will be forever expanded, allowing you to reach further, and go further than you thought possible. Every time you expand your comfort zone, your self-confidence and self-esteem expands as well. Once you make this a practice, and feel the boost in confidence, stretching outside your comfort zone will be exciting, and something you look forward to doing!

> *Do one thing every day that scares you.*
> – Eleanor Roosevelt

Implementing the strategies in this book, and particularly this chapter, will assist you in managing your energy to keep it exactly where you need to be without burning out. With every journey, the traveller is required to rest and rejuvenate. To recharge their batteries, not only physically, but emotionally and spiritually as well. Without learning to slow down or even take a short break on your path to your goal, burnout will surely prevail. Learn to power up and power down effectively, so you can reach your goals efficiently!

Chapter 6: Key Concepts

- There is no straight path to a goal.
- Most people are walking around with low energy because they are dehydrated.
- Your body will tell you how you feel about something before your mind has a chance to analyze it, put it through belief systems, and create thoughts about it.
- While in a relaxed state, creative juices flow easier and are unrestricted.
- Allowing an hour or two between screen time and pillow time will improve your quality of sleep.
- Positive energy equals productivity and progress.
- Power up with perpetual laughter!
- You will need to take risks and be uncomfortable in order to reach your goal.
- The more you naturally feel comfortable stretching outside of your comfort zone, the more successful you will be.

Chapter 7

Perfectly Imperfect

Being that you are human, you will not be perfect at anything. Sorry to burst aspiring perfectionists' bubbles! So, don't beat yourself up or get upset if you have oopsies, uh-ohs, or $%#*s. Be content to be perfectly imperfect. No one does anything great without making mistakes, getting thrown off track, or discovering they lost time, money, and energy, needlessly. Keep focused on why you want what you want and your successes along the way, so you will get to your goal. Anytime you feel unmotivated or stuck, simply ask yourself, "What are three ways my life will be better by taking action?"

Implementing the Homeplay activities, and what you have learned throughout this book, will act as the map and light guiding your path.

Riding the Ring

If taking steps towards what you want isn't enjoyable, your passion and willpower will fizzle out. As I have said before, there is no straight path to your goal. Life ebbs and flows, as will your attention, motivation, and the distractions that come into your life. Enjoy the ride of life, or what I like to call Riding the Ring. There are four stages of Riding the Ring. Riding the Ring is a circular, repeating pattern that happens with everyone no matter where they are on their path. The difference between people who are successful, and those that struggle, comes down to how they can manipulate the pace of the ride. The four points on the ring are: Chaos, Create, Care, and Complete.

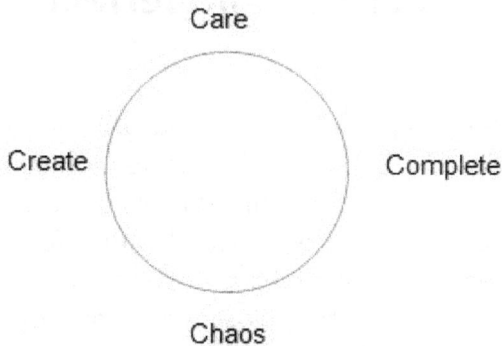

Care

Create   Complete

Chaos

For each stage, I will explain how life may look and what you may be feeling, how to move through each stage and avoid getting stuck, as well as practical action steps to take while in each part.

When in the state of Chaos, nothing seems to be going the way it is supposed to. You may spend a lot of your time putting out metaphorical fires and keeping your head above water. Life feels as though it is a struggle and a challenge. Signs that you may be in the Chaos stage are: your relationships may be strained, money may be going out faster than it is coming in, the to-do list gets longer than what feels manageable, and life in general feels really busy. During this stage, it is common to have a decrease in energy and progress, to easily get distracted, and to want to withdraw from life. The way to move through this part of the ring quickly is to do a preemptive strike. Metaphorically, break things up or destroy things that are creating unease and destruction. This might mean firing that employee that is bringing the team down, having a tough discussion with someone you are in relationship with, cleaning out the garage or closets to get rid of old energy and make room for the new, leaving a relationship that is not working, cutting up a credit card, throwing out all the junk food in your house, etc. While moving through the Chaos stage, look for ways to put a stop to the part of your life that is not working. Note: I am not suggesting that you give up on things or leave relationships just because you are in this stage. I give this suggestion ONLY IF you have wanted to do it for awhile and haven't taken action. Take action to remove that which steals your energy, time, money, and health.

After moving through Chaos, you will feel lighter and more energized. This is the time to Create. The stage of Create is exactly as it suggests: create, visualize, dream, and organize. While in this stage, create vision boards, look for lessons life has provided, explore new avenues and opportunities, plan your goals and action steps, and imagine your future. This stage is more about planning and preparing than actually doing. You may feel motivated and excited about all the possibilities that are at your fingertips. Creating is essential, but you do not want to get stuck with your head in the clouds. To move through this stage, set a specific time or deadline for you to create, and then be open to move to the next stage.

The next stage is Care. While in this stage, take time for self-care, relaxation, and celebration. This is my favourite part of Riding the Ring! It is time to stop and enjoy life. Many people speed by this stage because they are eager to get to the next step. Give yourself the gift of taking time to celebrate your successes and pamper yourself with rejuvenating activities. This may look like going to the beach for a day, taking a vacation, booking a spa day, having a party, getting together with friends, or having a pyjama day. Feeling serene, tranquil, and relaxed is good for your nervous system, mind, and overall well-being. Taking the time to renew and refresh yourself during this stage will no doubt prepare you for the Complete stage that comes next.

The fourth stage is Complete. During this stage, focus, attention, and momentum is what will transpire. It is the time in your life when you just feel on fire and make leaps and bounds towards your goal. This is when you will be motivated to take action steps and be busy DOING what it takes. It is natural to not be stuck in this stage too long, as eventually Chaos develops to restart the circle.

I share Riding the Ring with you to help you understand why it sometimes feels like you are on a rollercoaster of struggle and ease, of focus and distraction, and of progress and setback. Being aware of what stage you are in will help you to adjust your action steps to minimize unnecessary stress and strain. If you are in Chaos, it is easier to surrender into it than to waste energy and time trying to fight to focus on completing tasks or relaxing at the spa. Trying to relax at the spa, while you are in Chaos, will feel like your mind is over-analyzing or racing, resulting in you not being able to enjoy the experience. This will, of course, have you feeling frustrated and ultimately keep you in the state of Chaos longer. This is not to say you can't take a break to relax while you are in other stages of the ring! Just be aware of where you are so that you can make the best use of your time and energy.

Peace is the result of retraining your mind to process life as it is, rather than as you think it should be.
– Dr. Wayne Dyer

My Morning and Evening Rituals

Everyone will have their own preferences of the way they like things to be done. Take what works for you in this book and use it, modify it, and make it work for you. The 5 R's: Reason, Relationship, Re-Write, Repeat, and Rest and Rejuvenate, are the pillars and foundation to create the lasting changes you need. Just like building a house, a strong foundation will make the house last for years to come. Choosing to start building walls on sand is a blueprint to failure; although there really is no such thing as failure, if you choose to see it as feedback. Thomas Edison "failed" 10,000 times before he successfully invented the lightbulb. Fortunately, he chose to see it as feedback to improve what didn't work and try different ways.

I have not failed, I've just found 10,000 ways that won't work.
– Thomas Edison

Work towards your goal with the intention that you will see each setback, mistake, or failure purely as feedback. Use the information to create new ways of moving along your path. If you see failure as a stop sign, you will never reach your goal.

There will be perceived failure on your journey in your life and towards your goals; what you choose to do with it will either make you successful or stuck.

There is no failure. Only feedback.
– Robert Allen

I am going to share with you my rituals that I do to start and end my day. Did I just wake up one morning and automatically incorporate this into my routine? Absolutely not! I wouldn't expect that from you either. Start off with one or two activities that really resonate with you and increase from there as you become consistent.

I have never been known to be a morning person. For those of you that know me, I can hear you laughing at that understatement! My kids are my greatest teachers and guides. As they started getting older, I wanted to start their day off with positivity and happiness, instead of negative energy being thrown at them. This required me to shift out of my Eeyore "woe is me" cloud of negative, grumbling energy. For many, I am sure this can feel like an impossible feat. I used to wake up to a loud and severely annoying BEEP, BEEP, BEEP! Since I repeatedly hit the snooze button until the last possible minute before being late for work, I thought I would be clever and move the alarm clock across the room. My logical mind figured that if I had to get up out of bed, I would just stay that way. Nope! I just crawled back into my warm, cozy bed anyway. Every time that alarm clock would go off, I would feel increasingly annoyed, angry, and depressed. What a way to start the day! Unfortunately, I found those feelings would last throughout most of my morning.

This is what I do now to create positive energy in my mornings. I have two alarms that I set, neither of which involves a beeping noise that I can only assume was invented by someone out for revenge. My first alarm gently wakes me up to relaxing spa music or the sounds of nature. This allows me to gently bring my awareness into my room and think of all the things I am grateful for. I do this for as long as I choose to on that day. Some days it is for only a few seconds, but, on others, my gratitude space is for several minutes. At the end of this time, I say, "I love my life!" Saying "I love my life" was a practice I learned from Adam Markel, CEO of the personal transformation company, New Peaks. When I first started saying it, I felt uncomfortable, and that it wasn't quite true. When I incorporated it after focusing on everything I was grateful for, it quickly felt true and powerful. How could I be grouchy and negative, if I was grateful and loved my life? I couldn't!

If you find yourself falling back to sleep, or think that you would sleep right through that calming alarm, that is what the second alarm is for! (Although, I am almost always awake now before it goes off.) This alarm plays a soft song that I find uplifting, and slowly transitions into music I enjoy dancing to. Occasionally, depending on my activities that day, I may wake up to a hypnosis audio instead. However long the audio is, I set my alarm to begin playing the audio for that amount of time before I need to get out of bed. It feels great to start the day after listening to 30 minutes of positive affirmations! The reason I love listening to my hypnosis audios is, if I fall back to sleep, I am still getting the benefit, as the subconscious mind is always listening.

When I sit up on the side of my bed, the first thing I see is my vision board. A vision board is a display of words, pictures, and objects, that represent what you want to be, do, or have. I strongly recommend you create one as well! Because I enjoy moving slowly in the morning, I can productively sit and look at my vision board to remind myself of my goals and dreams. Focusing on my goals gives me a boost of energy and determination, creating momentum to take steps and make progress towards achieving them. In my notebook I keep beside my bed, I write down five intentions for the day that will help me get closer to my goals. These vary from to-do type items as well as how I want to be or feel during the day. For example, at one point in time, dropping my children off with my ex-husband felt unsafe and uncomfortable. One of my intentions those days was to take a few minutes before we met to think of all the positive attributes about him, or benefits of my children going to see him. Once in that positive energy and mindset, seeing him became less of an ordeal, and I would be able to check off completing that intention at the end of my day. I ensure to incorporate areas from every part of my life to keep balanced. I have goals for the following areas in my life: physical, intellectual/mental, spiritual, financial, social/relationships, professional and personal development. Obviously, I do not focus on every area of my life every day. If I find that I have been spending a lot of energy towards one area, I may consciously choose to focus my intentions on another area to establish balance.

After writing my intentions for the day, I feel inspired. I then walk into my bathroom and I am greeted with positive affirmations on my mirror. While getting ready for the day, I can read the affirmations and feel my energy expanding. Listening to positive, upbeat music has my feet tapping and body grooving as I get ready. I end this process by declaring, "I love and approve of myself," as I look myself in the eyes in the mirror. By the time I walk out of my bedroom to greet my children, I feel energized, on purpose, and enthusiastic! I'll be honest. This is not the case every morning, but the days of storm cloud mommy are few and far between. My children know that my time getting ready is 'mommy's alone time' to do self-care. I am pretty sure they have connected disrupting my morning routine equals unhappy mommy, so they are respectful. The rewards of smiling, happy children going off to school is reward and motivation enough for me to continue these simple tasks.

Long ago, I stopped listening to and watching the news, which mostly focuses on what is wrong in the world and breeds negative energy. I also save my social media and other screen time until later in the day. If something really important is happening, do you think I still find out about it? Of course! Our family has not had a subscription to television for years now, yet we still know all the major events that happen in the world. I don't believe we are ostriches putting our heads in the sand to avoid everything that is going on in the world. The negative energy of repeatedly watching crime and tragedy does not accomplish anything in my opinion, except to make people depressed. While visiting my grandfather in the senior community living complex he was living in, I noticed he always had the news station on. I started to become aware of the inordinate amount of negative stories there were compared to how many positive ones were being aired. No wonder he, and many of the residents there, were depressed and sad!

Integrating these rituals into your morning routine takes virtually no extra time. I like that they are already set up for me, so I don't have to think about it or expend time or energy preparing. They serve as a constant reminder of how I want to feel, what I want to achieve, where I am headed, and who I want to be. Like anything, once we see something repeatedly, we stop paying attention to it. To consciously do these activities, I change the look of my vision board, and my affirmations, frequently. On my vision board, I move items around, put new powerful words up, put the focus around a different area, use different colours, etc. I change my affirmations to be applicable for whatever I need to focus on or feel for the events in my life at that particular time. Sometimes I take down my affirmations and put up my list of reasons why I am working towards my goal. Being reminded of my reasons keeps me focused on choosing steps throughout my day that will get me closer to my goal. When I set the goal to release weight, for example, reading my list first thing in the morning, of the reasons why I wanted to be lighter, encouraged me to make a healthy smoothie for breakfast instead of having toast. I felt better all morning because I had started my day with a healthy choice. Since success breeds success, I frequently continued my healthy choices throughout the day, boosting my confidence and self-esteem. On days I ate unhealthy for breakfast, it usually ended in a downward spiral, as I had already 'wrecked' that day.

I have found morning routines to be most beneficial and valuable, as the positive energy is carried throughout the day. My intention for you is to create a practice that is simple, powerful, and quick. If you are finding you are taking an hour or more to do your morning or evening routine, you may be setting yourself up for sabotage. In the evening, my rituals and routines are very simple as well. My evening rituals vary more than my morning ones, as I choose the activities that most connect with me at that moment.

Once in bed, I review my intentions for the day and check off which ones I completed. If I have intentions that I did not complete, I take a few minutes to reflect on why, and what I could do differently next time. In my success journal, I write at least five things I accomplished or was successful at that day. Some days, it feels like the only thing I can think of is I made it through the day. As I look deeper though, there are always plenty of things that I accomplished.

If it is my day to check in with my accountability buddy, I update them on my progress at this time. On days where I have something special to celebrate, I will share it with my accountability buddy and at least one other person. Often, I will write in my gratitude journal what I was grateful for that day, especially on days that felt particularly challenging. The key to this is not just absentmindedly writing things down, but to feel what it feels like to actually be grateful for those things. I like to look back over what I was grateful for in past months and years. I always feel my energy shift. It helps me gain perspective and appreciation for everything that has happened in my life. If I feel overwhelmed, or like there is a lot on my mind, I may journal to unload all my thoughts or get clarity before going to sleep. Most nights, I spend at least half an hour reading a personal development book that is associated with an area I am focusing on. Maybe you do this as well and that is why you are reading this right now! Ending my day in an inspired and grateful space is so relaxing and comforting—the perfect feelings to have when laying my head on my pillow. As I turn my light out and start my hypnosis audio, I take three deep cleansing breaths. These three deep breaths serve as an anchor that puts me to sleep until morning. My evening routine can take anywhere from fifteen minutes to an hour, depending on how much time I have allowed myself and what I feel will be most supportive.

How will you create your life?

Success is the sum of small efforts,
repeated day-in and day-out.
– Robert Collier

Homeplay: AM/PM Tuning

Time: 15 minutes

Purpose: To create morning and evening routines that will get you powered up or powered down, refocus your energy, and keep you connected to your goals.

Materials Required: Paper and Pen

Exercise:

1. Create a morning routine that will get you into the energy and focused mindset to be consistently ready to play full out in your life. Make sure this is something that is doable on a consistent basis. Don't write that you will get up and go to the gym every morning if you struggle to get out of bed to get to work on time now. That may be a long-term routine you want to incorporate, but set yourself up for success now. Maybe, for

right now, the goal could be getting out of bed 10 minutes early to stretch your muscles. As that becomes automatic, stretch your comfort zone a little more.

2. Create an evening routine that will help you positively reflect on your day, unload your worries and concerns, and anchor you into falling asleep when you are ready. Again, set yourself up to thrive. If there are too many things to do, or it takes too long to complete all the tasks, you will eventually give up and stop.

Takeaway:

Having a set routine that becomes a ritual and just part of what you do, is something that will keep you in the energy and mindset to achieve your goals. Use the 5 Rs as pillars to form your activities around. Have fun and experiment! Be open to change, so change will occur.

All these tools, techniques, and information are useful, but it doesn't mean anything if you don't apply it. Knowledge is nice, but application is power. There is no such thing as a quick fix. Consistency and implementation is key. This book is about creating habits to achieve your goals easily. The only thing holding you back from your goals is you. Once you get your head and heart on board, there is nothing impossible.

"Vision-> Commitment-> Action= Results" – New Peaks

Homeplay: Future Unfolding

Time: 10-15 minutes

Purpose: To be aware of what your life will look like and feel like if you do nothing to change.

Materials Required: Paper and Pen

Exercise:

1. Write how your life (health, family, relationships, finances, spiritual, etc.) will unfold in the next one, five, ten, or twenty years, if you *do not* choose to make the required changes in your life. Be creative and really feel in your body how that will affect you.

2. Write what your life (health, family, relationships, finances, spiritual, etc.) will be like *when you do* make the changes you seek. Be creative and really feel in your body how that will affect you.

Takeaway:

Often, we do not take the time to think about how our decisions affect our lives. One day runs into the next, and soon we are a year or two down the road and nothing has changed. This Homeplay activity not only gives you the opportunity to imagine and feel what it will be like to be successful, but also how it will affect other areas of your life and those closest to you. Imagining what life will be like if nothing changes, can be motivation enough to take action.

If you are willing to do what's easy, life will be hard. But if you are willing to do what's hard, life will be easy.
— T. Harv Eker

Well that was awesome, now what?

If you have done all the Homeplay activities and read this far, you have set yourself up with the 5 Rs for success. Now what? Do you feel like a baby bird being pushed out of the nest, hoping you will fly to success? You may feel like you have got things under control and are ready to soar, but what happens when you hit turbulence? Maybe you are so energized you want to share what you have learned with others. Here are three of my favourite ways to share the wealth and create connection with positive people.

Mastermind

In Chapter 3, I discussed the importance of quality relationships and accountability buddies. So, how do I form this type of support, you may be wondering? The first step is to identify the type of goal you want to work towards. This could be weight release, business development, parenting, relationships, financial freedom, or whatever your topic of choice. The next step is to brainstorm people you know, or places where you could find people that are working towards the same or similar type goal as you. They must have the qualities of someone you want to work with, such as dedication, commitment, open-mindedness, and the capability of supporting others. You may come up with your own list of qualities for your group. The next step is to have a brief conversation with each person to see if they would be interested in learning more about how a Mastermind could benefit them.

A Mastermind is one of the most powerful forms of supportive relationship. The main objective is to create a metaphorical hula hoop of heaven around you, consisting of people who make it feel as though anything is possible, who reinforce your worthiness and capability of reaching your dreams and desires, and who fill the group with love and respect. Living in a hula hoop of heaven will change your life and make it feel as though anything is possible. Masterminds are simply groups of likeminded people coming together with a common goal of holding each other accountable and creating solutions bigger than themselves. When the group gets together, generally on a monthly basis, each person will take a turn sitting in the hot seat. The hot seat is an opportunity to share what the person is working towards and the obstacles they foresee or are experiencing. It is also important at this time to explain why their goal is important to them. They will then ask the group for support and/or resources to assist them in breaking through resistance, sabotage, obstacles, and whatever else they may be experiencing. The hot seat member will not go into background stories, excuses, or explanations, as they only have five minutes to share. A designated group member will be responsible for timing each section of the meeting, so the meeting ends on time.

The group will then have 30–45 minutes to support the hot seat member and respond. The first couple of minutes is for the group to ask clarifying questions to make sure they fully understand what was presented. The next 5–10 minutes is to ensure the goal has all the qualities required to make it achievable. Is the goal realistic/achievable? Is it measurable, meaning the person will know when they have reached the goal? For 15–20 minutes, the group can brainstorm ways of overcoming obstacles, alternative paths to achieve their goal easier, and offer resources such as books to read, people to see, personal support outside the meeting, etc. During the brainstorming section, the hot seat member is only listening and contributing ideas. They do NOT criticize, reject, or eliminate ideas at this point. There will be a person from the group designated to record all the ideas and commitments other members of the group offered to give the hot seat member at the end of the meeting. The last 10–15 minutes is set to create an action plan for the hot seat member. This could involve setting deadlines and chunking tasks down into daily, weekly, and monthly stepping stones. At the end, the hot seat member will thank the group for their support, and state their new goal with a date to be achieved by.

After speaking with people on your list about Masterminding, invite those who are interested, and have the qualities you require, to your house for an evening of conversation and a brief demonstration of how the group will operate. You may need to spread this out over two or three separate nights, depending on how many people you have on your list. Each night should have no more than ten people attending, so you can see the dynamics and interactions of each potential member. By the end of these evenings, you will want to narrow down the group to no more than ten committed members. Even though every member shows interest, it does not mean they are automatically enrolled in the group. You are the gatekeeper and will only allow people who are truly ready to support others on their journey and be willing to receive feedback themselves. They need to embody your ideal member attributes and characteristics, or the group will experience many struggles. Six quality members is better than ten members with four out to highjack the group.

Great minds discuss ideas; average minds discuss events;
small minds discuss people.
– Eleanor Roosevelt

Alan Deutschman, in his book, *Change or Die*, discusses several studies of people's inability to change. One study discussed the findings of Dr. Edward Miller, at Johns Hopkins University, regarding the rate of success heart disease patients had after having surgery to unclog their arteries. They were told by doctors that to keep from requiring further surgeries, and to avoid pain, they would be required to change their lifestyles to incorporate healthier habits. Even after literally being told to change or die, only 10% of the patients made a significant change to their lifestyle. This means that 90% of people, 9 out of 10, after having surgery, did not make the necessary changes to improve their health. Dr. Dean Ornish, at the University of California, conducted an experiment with patients that had clogged arteries and qualified for bypass surgery. Instead of having surgery, however, he had them change their lifestyles to healthy habits such as quitting smoking and eating a vegetarian diet. The patients were also required to participate in group meetings twice a week and take stress management classes like yoga, meditation, and exercise. The study lasted one year. Upon checking in with the patients' progress two years after the study ended, 77% of the patients continued implementing the healthier lifestyle practices. Support of likeminded people is key to success.

Stop Quitting on Yourself Book Club

Another way to connect with people is through a book club. Book clubs do not require that everyone be working towards a similar goal, although that is ideal. The structure of the club is very flexible, depending on the needs of the group. Some groups may decide to meet weekly, while others prefer to meet once a month. I suggest bi-weekly get-togethers. This gives everyone enough opportunity to read the designated section, prepare answers to the questions, or form their own questions. On my website, lightenuptherapy.ca, you will find discussion questions to use when reading this book with other people as a book club.

Facebook Groups

To get ideas, support, and stay connected to the information in this book, please join our Facebook group page www.facebook.com/stopquittingonyourself. On this page, you can ask questions and get ideas from other members, as well as be connected with other resources to keep you learning and growing.

The only place where success comes before work
is in the dictionary.
— Vidal Sassoon

Resources

Throughout the book, I refer to companies, people, courses and books that have guided me in my personal and professional development. Here are some of those resources and a few others that I recommend to increase your awareness, knowledge, and, ultimately, your success!

Resources related to Physical
Books:
You Can Heal Your Life by Louise Hay
The Myth of Mental Illness by Thomas S. Szasz
Selling Sickness by Ray Moynihan and Alan Cassels
Overcoming Thyroid Disorders by Dr. David Brownstein
Wheat Belly by William Davis M.D
Video:
Food, Inc.
Forks Over Knives
Hungry for Change

Resources related to Spiritual
Books:
The Monk Who Sold His Ferrari by Robin S. Sharma
Conversations with God by Neale Donald Walsch
The Untethered Soul by Michael A. Singer
The Science of Miracles by Gregg Braden
The Shadow Effect by Debbie Ford
Video:
What the Bleep Do We Know?

Resources related to Financial
Books:
Rich Dad Poor Dad by Robert Kyosiaki
Think and Grow Rich by Napoleon Hill
Secrets of a Millionaire Mind by T. Harv Eker
Course:
New Peaks: Millionaire Mind Experience
The Creators Code: Financial Freedom

Resources related to Relationship
Books:
The Five Love Languages by Gary Chapman
Calling in the One by Katherine Woodward Thomas
Non-Violent Communication by Marshall B. Rosenburg
The Queen's Code by Alison A. Armstrong

Resources related to Personal Transformation
Books:
Feel the Fear and Do It Anyway by Susan Jeffers
Ask and It is Given by Esther and Jerry Hicks
The Dark Side of the Light Chasers by Debbie Ford
Reframe Your Blame by Jay Fiset
Live an Inspired Life by Rae-ann Wood-Schatz
Awaken the Giant Within by Anthony Robbins
The Power of Intention by Dr. Wayne Dyer
Change or Die by Alan Deutschman
7 Habits of Highly Effective People by Stephen Covey
Radical Forgiveness by Colin Tipping
Video:
Genius Mind by Paul Scheele
The Secret by Rhonda Bryne

Course:
New Peaks: Reignite
The Creators Code: The Gift, The Launch, Accountability Intensive, Mastery Meaning and Mission
College of Professional Hypnotherapy Certifications

Resources related to Family Goals
Books:
7 Habits of Highly Effective Families by Stephen Covey
How to Talk so Kids Will Listen and Listen so Kids Will Talk by Adele Faber and Elaine Mazlish
Five Love Languages of Children by Gary Chapman and Ross Campbell

Chapter 7: Key Concepts

- Be content to be perfectly imperfect.
- Take action to remove that which steals your energy, time, money, and health.
- There is no such thing as failure, if you choose to see it as feedback.
- If you see failure as a stop sign, you will never reach your goal.
- Create a practice that is simple, powerful, and quick.
- Be open to change, so change will occur.
- Knowledge is nice, but application is power.
- Support of likeminded people is key to success.

That's a Wrap

You now have the tools to take the helm of your ship and set sail into the sunset. I love to hear how this book has helped its readers and those around them become the Captains of their own lives. Please share your success story with me through email or on our Facebook page. Reach out for support to assist you in surpassing your current reality. I sincerely wish you lots of success in your life. The life of your dreams and desires is waiting for you, so stop quitting on yourself!

The real risk of change isn't that you might try and fail.
It's that you might not try and you'll regret it.
– Adam Markel

Appendix A: Feeling Words

Amazed	Elated	Powerful
Animated	Enthralled	Proud
Aroused	Exuberant	Passionate
Astonished	Expectant	Pleased
Absorbed	Enlivened	Quiet
Appreciative	Fulfilled	Respected
Awed	Fascinated	Radiant
Accepted	Giddy	Rapturous
Alert	Grateful	Relieved
Amused	Glad	Rested
Blissful	Hopeful	Restored
Confident	Happy	Revived
Curious	Interested	Safe
Calm	Intrigued	Secure
Clear-headed	Involved	Stimulated
Comfortable	Important	Surprised
Centred	Inspired	Satisfied
Content	Invigorated	Serene
Courageous	Joyful	Strong
Dazzled	Jubilant	Thrilled
Delighted	Liberated	Thankful
Eager	Lively	Touched
Ecstatic	Loving	Tickled
Energetic	Moved	Tranquil
Excited	Mellow	Trusting
Engrossed	Open	Tenacious
Enchanted	Optimistic	Vibrant
Entranced	Peaceful	Warm
Enthusiastic	Playful	

Acknowledgements

The feeling of gratitude is one of my favourite states of being. I feel overwhelmingly grateful for the following people who have shared their knowledge, expertise, encouragement, inspiration, and support in my personal development journey thus far, and, of course, influence in the writing of this book. I am honoured to have had connection with you and will be forever grateful for your gifts and precious connections.

Thank you Jada and Edwin for allowing me the space and time to fulfill my dreams, as well as the unconditional love and acceptance you continually share.

Thank you to my dad for being a role model of humility, perseverance, and sacrifice, and for exemplifying the true meaning of family. I am proud to call you my dad.

Thank you to my hot rod Baba for teaching me about kindness, generosity, and having fun. May I lighten up the old folks' home as well as you do when I am your age.

Thank you to Dr. Jennifer Alexander for answering my many questions over the years, sharing your passion for hypnotherapy with the world, and believing in me even when I didn't.

Thank you to Jay Fiset for sharing your brilliant business brain and entrepreneurial gifts. Without your teachings of personal accountability and the Creators Code programs, I don't think I would have survived my 29th year.

Thank you to Rae-ann Wood Schatz for creating a safe space to be vulnerable and raw, while I shed the layers of my false self. Thank you for guiding me to uncover and illuminate my inner diamond. The experiences in your classroom, and as a part of your team, hold a very special place in my heart.

Thank you to Adam Markel and New Peaks for your high energy, high impact transformational programs. I am proud to call myself an enlightened warrior and apply those teachings into my daily life. AHO!

Thank you to my clients for sharing your journey with me. I am grateful and honoured you put your trust in me.

Thank you to John P. Smith Jr. for the inspiration to write this book. I never would have started without you sharing your contagious energy and experience.

Thank you to all my friends and family that have had any part in helping me become who I am today. Especially to those of you who provided invaluable lessons, that I did not see as lessons at the time. Your unforeseen gift that I did not truly open until much later in my personal growth journey is much appreciated, as I would not be the woman I am today without those experiences.

About the Author

Amber Howard is the founder of Lighten Up Therapy, a personal transformation company, offering Clinical Hypnotherapy, workshops, mastermind groups, and retreats. Her passion for helping people illuminate their inner being and creating their ideal life is evident in the quality of her work. Amber let fear control her for a majority of her life. This caused her to have poor relationships, missed job opportunities, financial struggles, and feelings of not being fulfilled. Through her research and development, she has transformed her thoughts, her behaviours, and her life. She now enjoys taking opportunities to stretch outside of her comfort zone and supports others to do the same. After experiencing the top five stressors (divorce, moving, having a baby, death of her mother, and starting a new job) within two short years, Amber learned how to thrive, not just survive. She has created transformational programming to help others change their habits, thoughts, and behaviours, so they too can create the life that they dream, desire, and deserve. Amber is the Chairperson of the Vermilion Crisis Line and Kids Help Line, and continues to work with youth in schools.

To book Amber Howard for coaching, speaking, or to attend her workshops, please contact:

info@lightenuptherapy.ca
lightenuptherapy.ca
1-888-950-4576

www.ingramcontent.com/pod-product-compliance
Lightning Source LLC
Chambersburg PA
CBHW071956090426
42740CB00011B/1960